Jumping the Border

In memory of my parents

Johnny and Tess

Could he speak English?, I asked him in Irish
— *An bhfuil Béarla agat?*
— *Bhí aon am, ach rinne mé dearmad air!*
—'Yes, I could once, but I have forgotten it!'

Séamas Ó Catháin interviewing
Pádraig Eoghain Phádraig 'ac a' Luain
at *Teach Eoghain Phádraig* in 1964

Jumping
the
Border

by

Séamas Ó Catháin

PHÆTON
PUBLISHING LTD.
—— Dublin ——

Jumping the Border

FIRST PUBLISHED IN IRELAND & U.K. 2018
by Phaeton Publishing Limited, Dublin

Copyright © Séamas Ó Catháin, 2018

Séamas Ó Catháin has asserted his right
to be identified as the author of this work

Cover & book design copyright ©
O'Dwyer & Jones Design Partnership, 2018

Printed and bound in the U.K. and U.S.A.

*British Library Cataloguing In Publication
Data: a catalogue record for this book
is available from the British Library*

ISBN: 978-1-908420-26-8 PAPERBACK
ISBN: 978-1-908420-27-5 HARDBACK

Contents

A Cub in Langfield

I CAME INTO THE WORLD between the two Christmases on New Year's Eve 1942 – Big Christmas and Wee Christmas, as they say. My birthplace was Drumquin in the parish of Langfield, County Tyrone. In those days, and even today to a large extent, where we lived was predominantly Catholic, but was an ecumenical sort of place in its own modest way long before that term came into fashion. The Parish Priest lived in the Parochial House hard by the Presbyterian church in what was generally thought of as the Protestant end of the village, while facing him across the Drumquin River was the Manse and the Minister, happily ensconced among his Catholic neighbours.

A local doctor doubled as registrar of births and so it fell to him to document the details of my arrival and take official note of my name. My parents' wish was to call me Seamus – the name I was given in baptism and which features on my baptismal certificate. My birth certificate tells a different story, however, for their declaration that I was to be called Seamus was brusquely dismissed by the registering doctor with a comment that Seamus was not a name, and James was entered on the official record instead. Years later, I would hear the poet, Seamus Heaney, recall a not dissimilar situation concerning the registration of his name, which officialdom rendered as 'Shames'.

Both first names followed me through life to the point I eventually opted for a name change by deed poll. To family and friends I was always 'Seamus' and in Irish-speaking circles I was generally called by the surname 'Ó Catháin' rather than 'O'Kane'. Officialdom only recognized me as 'James O'Kane', however, and it was in that guise I entered and graduated from Queen's University Belfast in the early 1960s.

Many years later, that registering doctor's colonial-minded intervention was rendered null and void when I enrolled for a higher degree at Queen's. With the encouragement and collaboration of Séamus 'Kit' de Napier, an Irish-speaking Belfast solicitor, the shift to Séamas Ó Catháin was speedily arranged; and my transmogrification (including an Irish-language spelling reform shift from *–us* to *-as* in 'Séamas') was complete.

My father, John (1908-1977) was a Langfield man through and through, the eldest son of James O'Kane (1878-1956) and Alice Gallagher (1880-1967), both members of families long settled in the parish. They married and made their home in Dooish, near the chapel and just opposite the parochial hall.

Granny and Granda (or 'Granga' as we pronounced it) O'Kane ran a modest country shop selling basic groceries, animal feeds, newspapers, tobacco, sweets, and minerals. They also kept hens and chickens and a few cows, sold milk to the local creamery and, like everyone else, made their own butter. The kitchen was a conventional spacious country kitchen of the time, dominated by a hearth fire with crook and chain and pots black with soot. To one side, a settle bed ranged under a small window facing across to a space where an outshot bed once stood, later converted into a small room where Granny lived out her long years of widowhood.

By and large, the O'Kanes were tone deaf, but the Gallaghers were musical and much given to dancing. Like many of her siblings and a houseful of cousins who lived alongside, Granny O'Kane was full of music. The complement of both homesteads ran into the low teens and, consequently, they never had any difficulty in finding someone to provide music for them and in making up a set for dancing.

Their house, like the adjoining shop, was thatched. I remember the excitement that attended the replacement in the early 1950s of the thatch by an ugly shiny corrugated iron roof – one of the first in the district. The family removed to a corner of what was called 'the tea-rooms', located beneath the parochial hall, for the duration, shifting for themselves there, cheek by jowl with the stables where Sunday Mass-goers arriving by pony and trap would tether their animals. 'Come on your *céilí*,' she would urge us children, 'and next time make a good *céilí*' (i.e. an extended visit). '*Céilí*' was one of the many Irish words both sides of my extended family still used freely. I was their first-born grandchild and looked upon with favour: 'What book are you in now, cub?' (i.e. 'what class are you in now, boy?'), Granda would ask almost every time we met.

Granda had at one time maintained a 'horse and van on the country', as it was described – that is to say travelling from house to house around the townlands of Langfield, selling groceries and other supplies from a horse-drawn covered wagon. Unfortunately for him and his family, he was foolish enough to engage in bartering goods for moonshine (rather than the customary butter and eggs) on too many occasions, became addicted to alcohol, and fell into debt. Fortunately, the business survived through the combined efforts of Granny and her first-born son, John, my father, who succeeded in rescuing the situation before it was too late.

My mother Teresa Cassidy (1917-1996), also a member of a big family, was born in the family homestead in Glengesh. The walls of their long traditional-style dwelling house still stand, perched on a steep hillside on the main road between Fintona and Tempo. Her sister Kathleen recalled that my mother spent her early infancy by the open hearth, nestling within a horse's collar to prevent her rolling over onto the hot coals. In the Loreto Convent primary school at Omagh she shared a classroom with the writer, Ben Kiely. Unlike him, however, she seemed to have formed little attachment to Omagh whose people she often described as being 'milk and water', whatever she may have meant by that. Perhaps she found them wanting when measured against the standards of her earlier life with its strong rural roots and continuing family links especially with her mother's people.

WEDDING PARTY OF JOHN O'KANE AND TERESA CASSIDY, 1941

My parents married in 1941, my father then aged 33 and my mother 24. They set up home in a house (where I was born) owned by a childhood friend, George Thompson. George and my father had both attended Dooish school, its complement of three teachers, one Protestant and two Catholic, roughly reflecting the confessional make-up of the surrounding community. My father always maintained that the Protestant and Catholic pupils who received their education in that environment fashioned bonds of friendship there that transcended sectarian boundaries and lasted throughout their lives. Such was the case between George and himself at any event. George, he said, was confirmed in the local Church of Ireland in a suit lent by my father to him for the occasion.

Both men had a strong entrepreneurial bent and were successful in establishing quarry businesses, mining the limestone rocks of Collow and Dunaree a few miles from the village of Drumquin. My father left primary school aged twelve or so and shortly after became a working-man with horse and cart and sledge, breaking stones and loading and delivering them for making roads. He often told how, once as he departed the family home in Dooish near the chapel at daybreak, he encountered a neighbour woman standing by the graveyard gate. He knew her well and wondered at her presence there at such an unearthly hour. His morning salutation to her was not returned and simultaneously he found extreme difficulty in controlling his horse which suddenly bolted, careering off at speed. On his return home that evening he learned that the lady in question had passed away during the night, the conclusion being that his early encounter had been with her shade and not the lady herself.

In due course, my father would acquire a lorry, then own a fleet of lorries and, at the height of his success, run a business employing upwards of thirty men. Alas, all of that was eventually destined to end in tears. Things were going well for him, however, at the time of his marriage to Teresa Cassidy in 1941.

My early education was at Drumquin Public Elementary School, a short trot over the bridge, up Main Street, and into what was unofficially dubbed 'Duck Street'. A schoolmate famously observed that Derry also had a Duck Street. He had seen it with his own eyes, he said, but his spelling left something to be desired, for it was of course not Duck Street, but Duke Street, that had caught his attention on that occasion.

I fetched up in Junior Infants under the strict eye of Una O'Kane of Dregish, who many years later married my father's brother, Pat. At the end of my first year, I won a prize – precisely what for I cannot recall, but I do remember the prize itself, a small rubber ball. I progressed to Second Class under an equally strict educationalist, a Miss Conway of Ballygowans near Omagh. My career at Drumquin P.E.S. ended before I fell into the clutches of Master Whelan, the headmaster, who ruled over the other end of the classroom in which we were taught. His energetic ministrations to the pupils in his charge were quite a distraction, especially when they engendered howls of pain. I was glad when my parents engineered my transfer to another school, the Christian Brothers Primary School in Omagh, where they felt I might be in receipt of a superior education. Alas, this turned out to be a classic case of jumping from the frying pan into the fire.

Drumquin Public Elementary School was a mixed establishment, by default as it were, for though it was under Catholic control, some Protestant children also attended. Our school was the nearest one to them. The only difference between them and us was that they were excused catechism lessons and instead granted the freedom of the schoolyard.

The signs of poverty were obvious to see all around us for many of the pupils were poorly clad, some spectacularly so. I remember one unfortunate lad being chased round and round the schoolyard, teased mercilessly all the while because of his unconventional mode of dress. The only covering he had to hide his nakedness was a ragged top-coat. Later in life, he became a successful politician and served on the local council for a spell.

DRUMQUIN P.E.S. 1947 – SÓC IN SECOND ROW, TWELFTH FROM LEFT

My recruitment as an altar boy happened during the curacy of Leo Deery, from Portstewart, whose energetic engagement with the life of the parish endeared him to one and all. He cut a dashing figure scooting about the place on his two-stroke motor bike. I accompanied him to what were called 'stations' in the country houses all over the parish, clutching before me on the pillion what was called the Mass box and hanging on for dear life. He was famous for organizing children's concerts in the parochial hall, as well as whist and 'twenty-five' card drives. After a while, he abandoned the bike and got a small saloon car in which he continued to dart around the place.

Once when travelling to Omagh he was halted by B-Specials

at a checkpoint along the way. They knew very well who he was of course but, just like everyone else, he had to state at gunpoint his name and render details of his itinerary. He duly sped on his way only to make a u-turn shortly after and come flying back the same way. So it went on, u-turn after u-turn, until eventually they tired of the whole business and waved him by without further interrogation. We deeply resented our neighbours, dolled up in their ill-fitting uniforms, questioning us at gunpoint, and revelled in our young curate's derring-do in ridiculing these local agents of the sectarian bigots at Stormont who ruled our lives.

Father Deery taught us Latin, or rather the Latin responses which we learned off by rote and gabbled from the foot of the altar: '*Ad Deum qui laetificat juventutem meam*,' we chanted, not understanding a word of it. Enjoying the chance to strike the gong at the consecration was a much squabbled-over privilege, as was lighting the charcoal and ministering to the thurible. The first time the latter task was entrusted to me, it nearly caused my grandfather to suffer a heart attack as I gripped the thurible with one hand and began swinging it mightily by its long chain. I came perilously close to completing the circle at times, no doubt with potentially disastrous consequences. Afterwards, the poor man made a point of telling me how it should be done, shortening the grip and using both hands.

Father Deery left me no less discommoded on another occasion when he asked me to accompany him on a trip to Belfast. My parents duly notified, I sat into his car to find he already had a passenger crouched on the back seat. She was a teenage girl, a native of the parish and a distant cousin of mine to boot. I said hello and she responded briefly and then fell silent for the rest of the journey. Father Deery maintained a steady conversation with me about this and that, but made no attempt to include his other passenger. Eventually we arrived at the Good Shepherd Convent on the Ormeau Road in Belfast where I observed her being hurried away to whatever fate awaited her within. On his return, I asked the priest about the nature of the establishment in which she had been deposited. 'It's a home for wayward girls,' was the brusque explanation offered and there the matter rested. She was pregnant of course and had been smuggled out of the parish to have her child far from home and beyond scandal-giving range. I was just a pawn in the proceedings, an unwitting chaperone whose sole purpose was to shield the priest from scandalmongery.

Once, the parish priest of the day, a Father McCauley, called to our house in similar style. There was no passenger this time and the journey turned out to be considerably shorter in duration. We had hardly gone more than a few hundred metres when he suddenly asked me if I had thought of becoming a priest. I said I had not whereupon, without further comment, he made a u-turn every bit as expeditiously as any his young curate might have done, and I found myself back where I started in double-quick time.

Neither my mother nor father, while good and loyal Catholics, were pietistic or sanctimonious. That was not their style. They supported the Church, but were well capable of taking an independent view of things and blatantly ignoring the advice of clerics. The works of Patrick McGill, the Donegal author, was a case in point. Two of his books – *Children of the Dead End* and *The Rat Pit* – met with special opprobrium on the part of the clergy who roundly denounced them from the pulpit and forbade parishioners to peruse them. For all that, I remember copies of these works being passed around discreetly in brown paper bags in spite of clerical denunciation. These writings of 'The Navvy Poet', as McGill was dubbed, were popular for reasons seemingly beyond the ken of the clergy: in the case of the former book, the setting of most of its early chapters was the parish of Langfield itself, where, in or around the year 1900, McGill had been hired as a boy of twelve to work for a farmer called Joe Young (whom he called 'Bennett'); the latter book was set in Scotland where many a Langfield native had toiled and endured conditions similar to those McGill described. Both these books were critical of the clergy, of course, and *The Rat Pit*, in making reference to prostitution, introduced a soupçon of what later became known as 'sex'. Heady stuff!

Memories of my childhood days in the rented house across the river are vague, a circumstance that may mean they were as happy as childhood days are supposed to be. It was a privileged enough existence, at least by comparison with the lives led by the members of most other local families. We had a generator and were one of the few families who had electricity. We had private transport, and despite war-time and post-war rationing, we had plenty of fuel and plenty to eat. I suppose as a family we could have been classed as burgeoning *petit bourgeois*: my father successful in business and an employer of men; my mother an active young mother who, unusually at that time, had learned to drive, and together with my father played badminton in local competitions (including those taking place in Orange halls).

More or less every family made an Easter House at Easter time and, in my day, this was a widespread practice throughout the community. Essentially these houses were little makeshift shelters made of sacks and branches, often built into a bank, but sometimes also freestanding. They had provision for a small fire within and space to sit and were usually open to the front. On Easter Sunday morning we sat around while a potful of eggs boiled merrily on the fire and then ate as many of them as we possibly could. In my mother's day, they would dye the eggs by boiling them together with onion skins and she and her sisters would take care to trace their initials on the shells with tallow before placing the eggs in the pot. The end product would be pale yellow-coloured shells with the various initials clearly outlined on them.

Every Christmas in Langfield and in most, though not all, of the neighbouring parishes, the roads used to be crowded with mummers. Dressed in a variety of outlandish costumes, groups of hardy individuals travelled on foot over hill and dale, sounding horns in wild hullabaloo as they approached each dwelling house along the way in the winter darkness. Having politely asked for and been granted permission to enter, they would swing into action in the time-honoured way –

'Room, boys, room, give us room to rhyme,
We'll show yez some activity about the Christmas time.'

The mummers would then proceed to perform a rudimentary play which sported a cast of named characters, bearing such titles as Prince (or King) George and Prince (or Saint) Patrick, one of whom would be cut down only to be revived by a doctor, who administers a life-restoring potion made up of all sorts of imaginary ingredients –

'Once I was dead, but now I'm alive,

God bless the wee Doctor that did me revive!'

There was much else besides, but the yardstick by which the overall performance was judged was not the quality of the playacting nor the novelty of the rhymes the mummers recited, nor the clarity of their diction, but rather the virtuosity of the musicians and singers they had in tow. The show ended with the mummers whirling the womenfolk in a dance around the kitchen and the taking up of a collection –

'Money I want and money I crave,

If youse don't give me money I'll sweep youse all to your
     grave!'

– the chief extortioner would cry. They were a scary sight for youngsters as they pranced around, roaring out their lines; and no wonder that my father banned them from our house after they scared the wits out of my brother, Aidan, who developed a squint, it was believed, as a result. The mummers were only too glad to be paid off at the door and hurry on to the next house they had in their sights.

At intervals, the nearby Drumquin River would burst its banks and the area surrounding the house and outhouses would be completely submerged under several feet of water. It was not much fun for the adults, but my sister Sheila and I had great fun paddling around in a large tin bath while the floods lasted. The house which still stands, and is occupied to the present day by George Thompson's daughter Joy and her husband, had one serious drawback then that posed a constant threat to my mother's sanity, namely the presence of rats. She told me that the floor around the cot in which I lay as an infant child had to be coated on a nightly basis with a heavily glutinous substance tacky enough to stop a rat in its tracks, which she said it did on many occasions.

Shortly after the war, though materials of all sorts were in short supply, the building of a house was begun on a piece of land my father had bought hard by the village of Drumquin, and by the

DRUMQUIN, CO. TYRONE

year 1947 we had moved into our new home. It was a square, two-storey, four-bedroomed dwelling whose most remarkable, indeed only, redeeming feature was the hall and kitchen floors. These were done in terrazzo, a flooring material of stone chips set in concrete and given a smooth finish. That terrazzo floor was the 'talk of the country', that is to say, our own parish and surrounding area. I remember Granda Cassidy and his son-in-law, Dinny O'Hagan of Eskra (married to my mother's sister Bea), laying wooden floors and doing other carpentry work while I played under their feet fashioning toy lorries from off-cuts of timber, with wheels made of shoe-polish-box lids.

The year 1953 marked the beginning of the sequence of events that led to the reversal of fortune that left my father close to bankruptcy. That year saw the unveiling of a war memorial in Pettigo, where Republican forces had fought a rearguard action, surrounded by elements of the British and Irish Free State armies in 1922. Four men died there, two of whom were Langfield natives – Bernard McCanny and William Kearney – and my father was one of many people involved in fundraising for the erection of a monument to those who lost their lives in that engagement. I was proud to see him on the platform in the summer of 1953 when the rather ugly statue of an Old IRA man, his rifle trained across the Donegal-Fermanagh border just a few metres away, was unveiled by Oscar Traynor TD, Minister for Defence in the

Irish government of the day. The huge crowd in attendance –
the biggest I had ever seen – thronged
the streets of Pettigo, overflowing across
the border to Tullyhommon in County
Fermanagh.
All this occurred about the time
my father had embarked on a major
development of his thriving quarry
business. He elected to switch to electric
stone-breaking machinery, a process
that necessitated bringing three-phase
electricity cross-country to the townland
of Collow in the hills above Drumquin
where the quarry was located. No doubt
that in itself was an expensive enterprise,

PETTIGO MONUMENT

but on top of that he was obliged to guarantee consumption
of power to the tune of no less than £900 per annum over
ten years in order to secure the deal. A working quarry
would have been capable of using such a sizeable quantity
of electricity with ease, but disaster struck when his long-
standing contract to supply stones to Tyrone County Council
was suddenly withdrawn and his business folded more or less
overnight. All through the war years, he had remained true
to his word, continuing to supply stones to the Council when
other quarries had reneged on their commitment in order to
enhance their capacity to supply materials for the construction
of St Angelo Airport near Enniskillen – an altogether more
lucrative venture paid for with American money.

My father's desperate pleading of his case fell on deaf
ears. Mr Glasgow, effectively what you might call the County
Manager of the day, told him again and again 'Mr O'Kane, my
hands are tied,' probably as clear an indication as that decent
man dared to give that politics rather than economics were
calling the shots. In effect, dominant Unionist power chose to
punish my father's 'disloyalty' (following his involvement with
the erection of the Pettigo monument), their disapproval of
him finding expression in quenching his light and throwing
his entire workforce out of work. It was a bitter blow, one

from which he never recovered. The breakers were sold and his fleet of lorries disposed of piecemeal at knockdown prices. Only the three-phase poles remained – as they do to the present day – a stark reminder of the crippling debt with which he was saddled for the course of the following decade. I well remember the arrival of quarterly bills, the last of each series emblazoned 'Final Notice'. Despite his straitened circumstances, the Northern Ireland Electricity Board continued to bill him to the end for electricity, not a single unit of which he ever burned.

The workshop in which his lorries had been serviced became a small garage drawing on the custom of the local community, an altogether far too limited market from which to wrest a decent living. Times were hard and even our daily bread was no longer guaranteed. Family meals often consisted of bread pudding, a soppy, unappetizing mulch of oven-baked leftover crusts of hard bread and milk, and little else. The entrepreneurial spirit that had sustained my parents survived to the extent that my father undertook the purchase of Maguire's drapery and shoe store with the aid of a loan from the Omagh branch of the Provincial Bank of Ireland. While that enterprise thrived, the garage business languished, barely able to pay for itself. Frequent recourse to drapery store income saved it from going under.

In the end, however, the drapery store, debilitated by shrinking financial resources, also began to suffer and eventually had to be put on the market. When no buyer could be found for it, my father's brother, Pat, stepped in and bought it for a song, later selling it on at a profit. The money it realized was insufficient to settle the bank debt and my father, pressed ever harder by an unsympathetic bank manager to cough up the balance, attempted to persuade him that his family would pay off the debt given space to do so. 'If you're relying on your family, Mr O'Kane, you're leaning on a rotten stick!' he was advised in no uncertain terms.

In citing the assistance his children might provide as a way out of the dilemma, he may well have been thinking of his own action in rowing in to save his father's grocery business nearly forty years before. He did not find us wanting, for all but one of us was either very modestly salaried or waged at the time and an arrangement was quickly put in place whereby, according to our means, we paid off his debt month by month until it was cleared. As soon as the last payment was made, all business with the bank ceased, much to the astonishment of the manager when informed by my brother Seán of our intention to switch without further ado to a rival establishment. 'We're no rotten stick,' was his Parthian shot to the baffled bank man.

My father developed heart trouble in the 1960s and was also afflicted with diabetes. The latter caused him to lose first one, then the other leg and, ultimately, these two ailments combined to claim his life at the relatively early age of 68. To distinguish him from many other O'Kanes he was called 'Big Johnny', not so much because of his height, but rather his girth. In his last years, as he struggled around on small rubber rocker legs, he was wont to refer to his former nickname, saying that he should henceforth be called 'Wee Johnny' instead.

He was good with his hands too and totally ambidextrous. I can picture him, a cigarette hanging from his lower lip, at work with his hammer, switching at will from one hand to the other as occasion demanded. My brothers Seán and Brendan inherited his good hands. My father, though thoroughly conventional in most ways, was remarkable for his skill in baking sponge cakes which regularly won him prizes at local shows. He had no compunction in exercising and demonstrating this unusual accomplishment.

After our parents' deaths, Seán would inherit the family home and the small portion of land around it at Omagh Road where he carried on the garage and also the funeral undertaking business that my father had operated as a sideline. Most of us were reluctant participants in one form or another in the operation of this business, Seán markedly more than the rest of us. Helping to seal coffins with bitumen and to stuff and line them with fabric was the least of our troubles; dressing and coffining the dead was more trying by far. My mother etched names and dates on the shiny plate with a special tool which she wielded expertly, before attaching the plate to the coffin lid.

Once, and thankfully once only, was I put in charge of a funeral when two such happened to coincide to the day and hour. I was deputized to preside at the less important of these and given detailed instructions as to how I should conduct myself. When the coffin containing the deceased was hoisted from the chairs situated on the 'street' outside the farmhouse door, it was emphasized that, on no account, was I to interfere if these chairs were 'tossed' – i.e. deliberately knocked over by mourners. They were to lie where they fell as the cortège moved away. Everything went well including the hazardous crossing of a 'kesh' (*ceis*) or 'footstep' i.e. a crude wooden bridge across a small stream that lay between the house and the main road.

My father's hearse was a thing of beauty, if vehicles of this sort may ever be described as such, for it was a converted Rolls Royce from, I think, the 1920s. It was a magnificent machine though unnervingly temperamental at times, not an ideal feature in the context of funeral processions. I got the odd chance to drive it home from funerals and rejoiced in exercising its

BRENDAN & JOHN O'KANE WITH THE ROLLS ROYCE HEARSE

'gate' gear change and practicing my double clutching technique. My father bought it in the early 1960s from a garage in Garvagh, County Derry, whence he followed me driving his car back to Drumquin. It cost him £100; the purchase of specially manufactured tyres for it cost him a good deal more than that, if I remember rightly. Years later, it was sold to a Rolls Royce buff for much more than it originally cost, tyres and all.

Langfield wakes were traditional affairs held in the

family home and generally lasted two nights. Protestants and Catholics were buried by undertakers of their own persuasion, but attended each other's wakes without friction or embarrassment of any kind. At my father's wake, I found myself sitting alongside an elderly man by the name of Willie Nethery, a member of the local Presbyterian church. He and my father were good friends and he cried softly as he told me of his sorrow at his passing. In politics, they had been deadly enemies, each separately charged with the duty of 'getting out' the vote, i.e. sparing no effort to ensure that every Protestant and every Catholic who had a vote (and, perhaps, on occasion, some who didn't) had the opportunity of exercising the franchise. Election after election, the quantum of votes on either side remained unchanged and the result never varied.

They worked assiduously against each other's interests in the lead-up to the elections and on election day itself. Then, Willie told me that, having done their very worst against each other, they would meet up in a local hostelry about four o'clock in the afternoon and have a quiet drink to celebrate their achievement, signalling thereby the cessation of hostilities and the resumption of normal neighbourly relations. This simple ceremony of reconciliation, Willie said, followed the custom established by himself and by my grandfather, James O'Kane, whose duties in this regard my father had inherited.

—II—

Jumping the Border

I HAVE RUN THE GAUNTLET of many borders in my time, but the border I grew up with at home in Langfield was far and away the most trying.

At one time, the nearest border crossing to us was at the village of Pettigo, which consists of a couple of small streets. The border between the Republic and the Six Counties (specifically between Donegal and Fermanagh) runs invisibly through the village at the mid-point of the town's two bridges. One summer Sunday in 1964 my father was driving a minibus-load of us to spend the day by the seaside at Fintragh beach just beyond Killybegs. We crossed into Donegal at Pettigo and pulled up at the Irish customs post, which stood almost within

THE BORDER AT PETTIGO, COUNTY DONEGAL

spitting distance of the British customs post in Fermanagh over the bridge we had just crossed. There, we had the great misfortune of running into the same breed of 'tin Hitler' I would often meet up with later.

First, all of us – including small children and an aged granny – were ordered to disembark from the vehicle so that it could be thoroughly searched. This swiftly unearthed a picnic basket safely tucked away under one of the seats, which was duly opened for inspection. The young officer's devotion to duty was duly rewarded by the discovery of a cache of eggs.

The eggs, he declared, would have to be confiscated as an illegal import. This prompted an outburst of bad language

17

from my father the like of which I would never have believed him capable. Among other things, the customs man was informed that he was 'no better than a f...ing B-Special', not a particularly apt image, perhaps, for a young customs man to contend with, who had probably only seen said species at a safe distance, but the meaning of which was well understood by us at least. The issue was finally resolved when the eggs were divested of their shells, showing them to be hard-boiled and therefore passed for importation.

This absurd episode perfectly illustrates the frustrations of living with an artificial border policed by little corporals that was the bane of our lives, dividing neighbours and families. It must be said that, taking fowl pest ordinances into account, the customs man was probably within his rights, but in that place at that time it would not have been hard to imagine hens and pullets scurrying back and forth across the border more or less under his feet – regardless of what the regulations stipulated.

Encounters with customs officers were a constant source of anxiety and, sometimes, considerable aggravation. Anxiety, because in the 1940s and 1950s especially, contraband in the form of butter, sugar, and other goods were smuggled at every opportunity from what we called 'the State' (the Irish Free State) into 'the Six Counties', the latter being the only acceptable designation we had for what is now generally known by nearly all political persuasions as Northern Ireland. By the same token, 'the State' was simply the name for the part of Ireland that lay outside the Six Counties. This was mostly deployed in phrases such as 'up somewhere about the State', meaning 'far to the south', most likely Sligo, Leitrim, Monaghan, or Cavan. Donegal, which was at home with us across the fields, was just 'Donegal'.

I remember a smuggling trip we made to the neighbourhood of Garrison in County Fermanagh and the family home of a friend. The family farm ran along the border with County Leitrim, somewhere in the hinterland of Kiltyclogher. We all trooped down to the river that divided the two counties and, crossing by stepping stones, made our way up to a house on the other side. There, stacked high around the walls of a large room off the kitchen were packs of sugar and cartons of butter, more that I had ever seen before. Purchase completed, we trooped back across the frontier, each armed with a burden of goods which we then concealed for further transport back home to Tyrone.

Concealment was very often the order of the day when we travelled home from seaside visits to Bundoran in County Donegal. At a certain spot, a few kilometres short of the border crossing at Belleek, County Fermanagh, the females on board, including my mother and her sister Susie, would disembark and disappear behind a wall by the roadside. They would re-emerge swollen like Michelin men, their clothing stuffed with all manner of perishables and, with the greatest of difficulty, they would squeeze back into the car to make the crossing. Safely on the other side a few kilometres down the road and with much laughter, loosening of 'stays' (corsets),

THE BORDER IN THE 1950S

and snapping of elastic, packs of sugar and butter would be disinterred from their hiding places.

Donegal was a cornucopia of other delights such as Aero chocolate bars, American comics, and triangular 'Three Counties' processed cheese, all of which were unavailable in the North at the time. In later life, I learned that packets of 'Spangles', a kind of fruit drop, were equally cherished by 'Free State' youngsters from the other side of the border where such delicacies were not to be had. Post-war rationing and the use of coupons controlled the purchase of all sorts of goods, including sweets, into the 1950s.

With the purchase of my first car, I became embroiled

in the tiresome business of acquiring the documentation that would enable me to travel back and forth to Donegal. I accomplished this with the aid of my father, a seasoned border tripper, who first steered me to an acquaintance of his in the border village of Lifford in county Donegal. The acquaintance agreed 'to go bondsman' for me, that is to say to formally guarantee that I would abide by the rules regarding temporary vehicle importation. If I remember rightly, he stood to suffer a loss of £200 if I did not. I thus became the proud owner of a passbook – a document which cross-border motorists were required to present to be stamped on entry and exit at the Irish border post. (The possibility of a body search was a constant threat, but this fate befell me on only one occasion as far as I recall).

If you happened to arrive at the border after the post had closed for the night (at varying times from about 9:00 PM) you had to stay put until the following morning

BORDER POST SIGN

or take the risk of 'jumping' the border. 'Jumping' the border one way meant that you had to 'jump' it back the other way in order to make a legitimate exit at some future point.

Alternatively, if you could find a telephone and rouse an operator – not a particularly easy task on either score – you could ring the nearest border post and 'put in a request', as it was called. This involved fixing a time for a customs officer to be present in order to process your passage, attached to which service there was the not inconsiderable fee, as far as my pocket was concerned, of two shillings and six pence.

I have a memory that different crossings operated different schedules, some remaining open longer than others and some, perhaps, opening longer at weekends or at other particularly busy times. I have a memory of my father having to adjust his route home from Donegal on one occasion when he realized that he would not reach the Pettigo crossing before closing time and consequently was forced to detour in order to cross at Belleek.

Other than the numerous 'unapproved' routes, only the border crossings at Belleek, Pettigo, and Lifford were available to us, each a gateway to various parts of Donegal: Belleek was the portal to Bundoran and also Sligo and the West; Pettigo led to Donegal Town and 'in through', as they say, to Killybegs and Gleann Cholm Cille; and from Lifford, one could make for Letterkenny, Fanad, and the Rosses, or strike due west to Ballybofey, Glenfinn, and Glenties.

Return journeys from Glenfinn to Tyrone meant taking the Lifford-Strabane crossing and, of an evening, keeping an eye on the clock with a view to meeting the deadline at the border or managing to 'put in a request'. Occasionally, Lifford offered an unexpected bonus in terms of customs availability, due to late-night dancing in the Orchid ballroom which drew a large cross-border clientele. The trick was to know which nights there would be dancing there as the customs post operated late opening then and you could save your money. One learned to keep a sharp eye out for poster advertisements containing relevant details of the Orchid's programme of dances.

When I was at Queen's in Belfast, a colleague introduced me to the piano accordion, and ultimately sold me his old 'box' when he upgraded to a newer model. Although I was never more than a mediocre exponent of the art of accordion-playing at any time, my modest talent enabled me to accompany singers (including myself), vamp for real musicians, and even play some popular rhythms and airs. I later bought a bigger and better machine from the same individual and, though somewhat the worse for wear after all these years, this old accordion (or 'JCB' as some unkind souls disparagingly call it) is still serviceable enough to be hauled out of its battered case for special occasions, of which there have been a good few over the years.

My accordion has been subjected to a variety of indignities in its time and had once been splattered with beer flung in anger at someone standing behind me in a Mayo pub. I cannot recall who the intended victim was but the perpetrator was a high-flying civil servant who later became the head of several different government departments. Thank goodness, the perpetrator was aiming high in more than one respect – otherwise my 'box' might have had to take early retirement,

More threatening by far was the officious attitude of a young customs man doing his duty on the border between Tyrone and Monaghan at Moy Bridge (Aughnacloy). In the days before the advent of the EU Single Market (in 1993) border crossings were strictly regulated by the British and Irish authorities. The verbal challenge 'Any goods to declare?' always drew a negative response – regardless of the circumstances. Returning to Dublin from a family function in Tyrone in September 1987, an investigation of my car boot revealed the presence of a battered accordion case which I was ordered to haul out and open by the roadside. I was then subjected to a rigorous cross-examination regarding the provenance and value of its contents by the officer concerned, who seemed to be convinced I was some class of accordion smuggler and appeared hell bent on seizing the 'goods' unless I could provide a receipt showing the date and place of purchase. Much to my relief, he eventually granted a grudging permission for the importation of my 'box' from Tyrone to Monaghan and all was well.

Once, I travelled from Dublin with some colleagues on a field-trip to collect folklore in Inishowen. We intended to make video-recordings of singers and storytellers there, but in order to carry the necessary equipment we were compelled to acquire a carnet which contained details such as camera serial numbers etc. for presentation to the customs authorities at the Monaghan-Tyrone border and, again, at the Derry-Donegal border.

All that sort of thing is gone now. I hope it will never return, but should it do so, I have no doubt a new corps of border smugglers will spring up eager to emulate previous generations in thwarting irksome and often petty regulations.

Nowadays, innumerable roads, big and small, and the lack of controls make crossing the border much easier than before and small-time smuggling has become a thing of the past, though various other kinds of large-scale commercial smuggling enterprises still thrive.

One fellow, it is said, used to turn up every day bold as brass at a border post, wheeling a bicycle with two large saddlebags. Needless to say, his daily appearance generated a degree of suspicion on the part of the customs officers who, day in day out, quizzed and body-searched him and diligently inspected his saddlebags only to find them stuffed with sand and concealing nothing. They were mystified but could pin nothing on him and allowed him to pass on every occasion. Years later, the cyclist met with a retired customs man who recalled his many encounters with him, saying that they knew very well that he was smuggling something but could never say what. 'Bicycles!' said he. This little story of the Tyrone-Donegal border is told in many countries across Europe and beyond, wherever borders are found.

BORDER POST INSPECTION, 1932 [*PHOTO: LEONARD PUTTNAM AP*]

III

'Felix Education'

MY TRANSFER to the Christian Brothers School in Omagh entailed a return journey morning and evening by bus, courtesy of the Ulster Transport Authority. Initially, we travelled in what were known as 'utility' buses – very basic vehicles with uncomfortable slatted wooden seats and little if any heating. The novelty of the ten-mile jaunt to Omagh faded quickly and going to school by bus became routine over the next nine years or so that I attended first the CBS Primary and then the CBS Grammar School.

The bus left for Omagh at 8:30 AM and returned to Drumquin at 3:45 PM, leaving only a narrow margin at either end for making it to school on time and, more importantly, getting to the bus station on time to catch the bus home. Some teachers seemed to take a delight in not dismissing us until the very last minute, leaving us to chase headlong for the number 96, down High Street and across Bridge Street, schoolbags flying behind us. Occasionally we were forced to loiter about the bus depot killing time until the next bus left at 6 o'clock. We passed the time watching sports fishermen testing their fly-fishing skills in the river Strule or the conductors and drivers playing quoits as they too killed time pending their next departure.

In the beginning, I and a very few others made up the small complement of pupils travelling to school in Omagh, but the proportion of schoolchildren to other passengers gradually increased to the point where they became the majority, and the 'Drumquin' bus became so crowded that the overflow was often forced to board buses travelling from Castlederg to Omagh at more or less the same time. We preferred our own bus, for though we were a mixed bunch – some headed for Omagh Academy (the Protestant school) and others for 'The

Brothers' (as it was called for short) or the Loreto Convent
Grammar School (the two Catholic second-level schools) –
we all knew each other. For all that there was no animosity
between us, the different groups tended to cling together,
our separateness underlined by the distinctive colours of
the uniforms we wore. We heartily disliked being forced to
board the Castlederg buses as they were mainly populated by
strangers, most of them Academy youngsters.

The driver of the 'Drumquin' bus was a decent man from
Dromore called George Knox who, on frosty mornings, often
called to our house for a kettle of hot water to help him get
his vehicle on the road. Occasionally, to our great delight, a
stormy night might bring trees tumbling down resulting in a
detour by back roads and delaying our arrival in Omagh, thus
providing us with a cast-iron excuse for being late for school.

Once we were ordered home early because of rising floods. We got home safely through waters that in places lipped the top step of the entrance to the bus.

I entered third class in the Christian Brothers Primary School where I took my place as the only boy not from the town of Omagh or its environs. The teacher, known as 'Ghandi', was no 'townie' either, but a man from my own place. He was a fellow passenger, commuting to school morning and evening as I did, but there was no communication between us outside the classroom. He was a strict disciplinarian inside the classroom and wielded a long cane with dexterity, swishing it through the air for effect at regular intervals as a declaration of intent. I am happy to say that I rarely fell foul of him.

I made friends with some of the Omagh lads and progressed with them through fourth and fifth classes, after which – following the 'Eleven Plus' examination – many of us transferred across the narrow passageway separating the CBS Primary and Grammar schools and became secondary school boys. Under the lean, ascetic-looking Brother who took charge of us in fourth class, an element of academic rivalry gradually began to emerge between some of my 'townie' friends and me.

The Brother in question ran his classroom with fanatical discipline which included a morning inspection at which each boy was expected to exhibit his rosary beads, a clean handkerchief, and to present for examination clean sets of fingernails. Failure to comply in every respect resulted in the immediate administration of punishment to those offending against the rule. We witnessed this at close quarters from our place in the queue at his desk, as those who failed the test were obliged to bend across his knees and absorb the force of his leather strap vigorously applied to their upturned bottoms. This zealot later left the order to get married.

One of the achievements of my early education had been the acquisition of a fine longhand style of writing in which I took great pride. I had become quite adept at this and, indeed, won prizes for my penmanship at the Drumquin Young Farmers' Association annual show. I was devastated when the demands of my later education included a forced conversion to shorthand. I had to abandon the decorous old-fashioned longhand and learn to write all over again in the new style called 'script'.

The academic highlight of my year in fourth class was the annual test which embraced all manner of exercises and ran for a whole week. A curious element of the week's activities sticks out in my mind to the present day. Towards the end of the test, the Brother passed around a brand-new batch of poetry books, ordering us to choose a poem and commit it to memory. After a period of intensive study, the books were gathered up again and one by one we stood up to recite our party pieces.

I turned out to be the only boy able to deliver a poem word perfect, a feat rendered possible by my having had the presence of mind to select one of the shortest items in the whole volume. Others might well have opted for a similar course of action, but must have balked at the title and subject matter of the poem by Hilaire Belloc. It was all about 'The Yak', a creature of which I had never heard and of the pronunciation of whose name I was not at all sure.

> As a friend to the children commend me the Yak,
>   You will find it exactly the thing:
> It will carry and fetch, you can ride on its back,
>   Or lead it about with a string.
>
> The Tartar who dwells on the plains of Thibet
>   (A desolate region of Snow)
> Has for centuries made it a nursery pet,
>   And surely the Tartar should know!
>
> Then tell your papa where the Yak can be got,
>   And if he is awfully rich
> He will buy you the creature – or else he will not.
>   (I cannot be positive which.)

My recitation of Belloc's poem did the trick, however, and may have been the crucial makeweight that eventually turned the scales in my favour in terms of the overall result. I won the competition by a handful of marks, surpassing the best of the townies in the process. 'The boy from the hill country above Judea,' as that Brother was wont to call me (a reference drawing on the song title 'The Hills Above Drumquin') had made it to the top! It was a grand feeling and I still remember racing home from the bus to tell my father standing at his workbench about how I had beaten all of my classmates into a cocked hat. I forbore to ask him to buy me a yak as a reward!

The Brother who next took us in charge in fifth class presented an altogether different appearance. Below his florid countenance, a rumpled, soiled soutane sat awkwardly on his squat frame. He was an inveterate smoker, his addiction sometimes leading him to cadge cigarettes from boys he knew also to be given to the weed. His obvious lack of physical fitness tempered somewhat his enthusiasm for using the strap, and for that we were grateful. Despite his failings, he was a likeable man. There was great humanity about him somehow.

On the other hand, his habit of squeezing in beside us on the narrow benches, ostensibly to illustrate some point or other, but all the while attempting to fondle us, won him few admirers. But he was an excellent teacher and set a furious pace, including additional Saturday morning classes designed to ensure a pass for as many of us as possible in the dreaded Eleven Plus examination.

Success guaranteed a ticket of leave for further education; failure would consign us to sixth class and the tender mercies of another Brother with a reputation for meting out spectacularly brutal punishment, and also for fondling. Through the door linking fifth and sixth classes, we became accustomed to hearing the thud of the leather beating down on outstretched hands. Occasionally, a glimpse might be caught of a boy spread-eagled across a chair at the back of the class, trousers round his ankles, his bare posterior hoisted to receive a hammering.

One became resigned to the prospect of coming under the lash sooner or later and when it sometimes did happen one tried to bear it with as much dignity as possible. I was one of the lucky ones who managed to escape the worst of the violence and other unpleasantness, mainly by applying myself diligently to my studies and otherwise keeping a low profile. Carrying home complaints to parents and other elders was pointless for such appeals were always met with the standard riposte that the strap would not have been resorted to unless the punishment had been deserved and there the matter would rest. In all likelihood, little credence would have been given to descriptions of sexual harassment had we had the wit or the words to describe incidents of that sort. Nor, in all probability, would anything have been done about it in any case.

All in all, the latter phases of my primary school experience could be best described as having been an endurance test rather than a serendipitous educational experience. I became inured to the notion that somehow or other education and violence went hand in hand, an idea to which both teachers and parents all seemed wedded in those times. I have few recollections of lighter moments, of which I imagine there must have been more than I can remember.

I can only assume that at some level all of this must have affected me to an extent. Should the callousness of the education process have rubbed off on those at the receiving end, my classmates and I would surely have been desensitized by the excesses we witnessed and experienced. For my own part, I managed to dodge the worst of it all and, in spite of everything, learned enough to qualify for entry to secondary school.

Eager as ever to learn, and decked out in a new uniform to face an unfamiliar phalanx of teachers and a new range of subjects, I embarked on the next phase of my education. If nothing else, the ambient atmosphere of violence with which I had already become familiar proved to be an excellent conditioner for what was to follow at this higher level where a small group of lay teachers, whose dedication to physical punishment seemed to know no bounds, was loosed upon us.

Irish and History were two of the new subjects encountered in my first days at Grammar School, both taught by the same teacher, a talented man in many ways, who also taught us English. He introduced himself by first chalking on the blackboard a menu of misdemeanours and concomitant penalties ranging from one to twelve slaps. Punishment for infringements against his rule would be delivered by means of a leather strap he called 'Felix Education'. This, we later heard it rumoured, had been stuffed with three-penny bits by a local shoemaker in order to render its effect on the palms of our young hands all the more telling. Pulling and twisting ears or cheeks while simultaneously dragging victims upwards from their school benches into a standing position we later found to be the preferred option of other teachers. 'Felix', we were told, was the Latin for 'happy', but the 'reign of terror' – the term another teacher frequently employed to describe the conditions under which we laboured in pursuit of knowledge – was anything but joyful.

I witnessed physical abuse almost every day of my secondary school days, but, once again, managed to escape the worst ravages of the system, falling victim to it only now and then. One such event occurred the day after my Granda O'Kane was buried in December 1956. As one of the local altar boys I had been deputized to serve his funeral Mass in the parish church. Such was the thirst for education in those days that, following the burial, I was immediately whisked away to school in Omagh in order to attend the remaining classes of the day. At my request, my father explained to the Principal the reason for my absence and this was duly noted. The next day, however, the French teacher demanded that I hand over to him the customary note from my parents explaining my non-appearance at his French class. My explanation of the circumstances, and invocation of the Principal's name in my defence, cut no ice and I was condemned to suffer the usual penalty for not having a note just for him – six slaps if I remember rightly.

To our great delight, this sad figure of a man often felt much too poorly after a night's drinking to bother about us, and was wont to spend his first class of the day groaning and spluttering out the window of the classroom. I gave up French at the first opportunity in order to escape further engagement with him. My treatment at his hands still rankles to this day.

We generally took our punishment without demur and would return to our benches clutching our hands beneath our armpits, and when seated again, immediately grip the iron bench frames to soothe our throbbing palms and assuage the pain. Some boys were tougher than others to the point of insolence, even daring their tormentors to do their worst. Others were less hardy and more inclined to openly register their suffering. One fellow who sat at the very back of the class carried this to extremes for, as soon as he was called forth for punishment, he would commence to shake and sob and eventually blubber his way up to the front of the class and all the way back after taking the hit. Everyone knew his form and not an eye would be raised to witness this humiliating process nor was a word spoken about it afterwards. I often think that in empathizing with his predicament we showed more humanity as a body towards a vulnerable classmate than did the educators who ruled our lives so cruelly.

At the opposite end of the spectrum was another boy who constantly locked horns with the diminutive wielder of 'Felix Education', whom I shall here call Larry Leather. This boy was as stubborn as he was intelligent, and also worldly wise in a way that set him apart from the rest of us. In later life, he succeeded in business and ultimately became an extremely wealthy man. Larry Leather and he fought each other to a standstill, bringing out the worst in one another. In the end, however, I believe the moral victory belonged to the boy who never yielded an inch to his pocket persecutor. Day in day out, his challenge to authority resulted in multiple slaps – usually six on each hand – being delivered from as high on tip-toe as Larry could stretch. Thereupon, as often as not, the boy would nonchalantly raise his hand aloft again and invite him to repeat the dose and Larry would promptly oblige by giving him another dozen 'biffs', as he was wont to call them, and these would then be ceremoniously 'banked' in his notebook. We silently cheered on our champion while marvelling at his apparently endless capacity to absorb punishment.

For all its omnipresent threat, school was not all about /

punishment; learning, which also entered the equation, was mostly an enjoyable experience, particularly with regard to the subjects in which I took a natural interest, Irish, English, French, Latin, History, and Geography among them. I was hungry to learn, but Science (later Physics and Chemistry), Algebra, Arithmetic, and Geometry (all three later dubbed Mathematics) held little attraction for me, and to say that I regularly failed to excel at them would be no exaggeration.

Later, in university meetings and debates, I would often hear the Christian Brothers castigated for their determination to inculcate rebellion in their pupils. Such charges were usually levelled by apologists for Unionism, the real target of whose criticism was Irish culture in any form and the teaching of Irish history in particular. They need not have worried, if my introduction to the subject of history as taught in Omagh CBS was anything to go by.

This came accompanied by elaborate charts illustrating the bringing of Christianity by Saint Augustine to a land – England – then occupied by Jutes, Angles, and Saxons. Saint Patrick and the coming of Christianity to Ireland did not deserve a mention as far as the syllabus dictated by the Northern Ireland Ministry of Education was concerned. Some of the Brothers would use an occasional free period to expatiate on aspects of Ireland's history which constituted the only thing approaching sedition they preached.

Likewise, in geography, I learned little or nothing about the island of Ireland, but could soon list by heart – and accurately map – the rivers of England. Curiously, in primary school I had already learned in fourth class the names of Irish counties and their principal towns. For Tyrone, the litany ran – Omagh, Dungannon, Strabane, and Cookstown – and so on for each county of Ireland, most of the details of which I have now forgotten. When it came to County Clare, Ennis seemed quite unremarkable for we had a townland of that very name at home, but for some reason or other the name of Ennistymon caught my imagination, perhaps because of its peculiar spelling and unpredictable (as it seemed to me) stress pattern.

English was little different, for there the syllabus *inter alia* focused attention on Wordsworth, Coleridge, Pope, Keats, and Shelley, the essays of Charles Lamb and, in a volume called *Adventures, and Encounters*, the war-time exploits of Winston Churchill during the Boer War in South Africa and other far-flung places.

Not unexpectedly, perhaps, Irish was an entirely different kettle of fish. My first acquaintance with this language in a school context had been at primary level where I picked up, by a process of osmosis, highly garbled and – linguistically speaking – utterly opaque versions of the 'Our Father' and 'Hail Mary'. This changed dramatically at secondary level where I had my first real lessons in Irish.

The first thing to say is that from the start I was eager to engage with the language, a feeling I got from my parents who, like many others, had attended Gaelic League classes in Langfield Parochial Hall (St Patrick's), winter after winter. I was allowed to go along on a number of occasions and I marvelled at the sight of a hall full of people clutching lesson books whose simple contents they chanted for the teacher. As far as I recall, he travelled by bicycle from Strabane, a distance of some 13 miles or 21 kilometres, uphill all the way.

Pedagogically speaking, it must have been uphill all the way for him too, for the inauspicious learning environment in which he functioned was unlikely ever to make fluent Irish speakers of many of the natives of Langfield. Neither did it – at least to judge by my parents who could never manage more than a few basic phrases. For them, despite their best efforts, it was a matter of regret that the language was, and always remained, a closed book.

Neither of my parents, nor indeed any of their neighbours, had any foundation whatsoever in the language, of course, not having had the opportunity of learning it at school nor even having heard it spoken by older people of the locality. The western and southern fringes of Langfield remained Irish-speaking longer than other parts, but the last vestiges of Irish had vanished by the early decades of the twentieth century. My Granda O'Kane's granny was one of the last, dying at the age of 99 in 1901. The only real Irish speakers in the parish by the time I came along were the sons and daughters of the Donegal Gaeltacht who had come in search of work, mostly hiring with local farmers, and sometimes marrying into the local community. In later years, I sought out their company and became more closely acquainted with many of these fine people, who manfully tolerated my first ham-fisted attempts to engage them in Irish conversation.

Among their number were two unusual individuals, one a man from Inis Meáin, a small island just off Bloody Foreland in the far north west of Donegal, the other a woman from the Rannafast area of the nearby Rosses. Susan Gallagher has long since gone to her eternal reward, and Jack McCullough – who lived on the small farm he owned that had been left to him by the Protestant master with whom he was once hired as a servant boy – has also recently passed away.

Susan never married, but opted nevertheless to settle in Tyrone rather than head further afield or return to her native place. She reared fowl for sale at her little house on the Cow Market in Drumquin and was known to one and all as 'Shusan' or 'The Rossie'. Many a time I stepped the road home with her from Sunday Mass in Dooish, listening to her crisp tongue of Rannafast Irish and trying to respond as well as I could all along the way.

The proud possessor of an old Ford Prefect car in later years, I returned the compliment, as it were, by inviting Susan to travel back

Coláiste Bhríde, Rannafast

to the Rosses with me to visit her people whom she had not seen in many years. By that time, I was well acquainted with Rannafast, having been a student at *Coláiste Bhríde* and at *Coláiste Phádraig* in *Loch na nDeorán*, hard by Susan's home place. I remember her telling me of the hilarious public reaction in the village of Annagry when moving pictures were first shown in the local hall. Apparently, at the sight of what appeared on the screen, the assembled company scattered in all directions, declaring that what they had witnessed – quite possibly Charlie Chaplin – to be no less than Old Nick himself!

My contact with Jack was intermittent, but as recently as a few years ago, I met with him on the roadside near his home where, in spite of his advanced years, he was busy making land drains. I stopped for a chat and we fell to talking about island life in Inis Meáin and how he had learned to row the truncated Donegal currach. His repeated pleadings with his uncle to let him take a turn at this eventually bore fruit and he was allowed to have a go.

This small, fragile craft is propelled by a paddler kneeling in the prow, the stern jutting high out of the water if not weighed down by a passenger seated on a bench at the rear. To illustrate the point, Jack fell to his knees on the grass verge and, wielding an imaginary paddle, set to, repeating his uncle's anxious instructions to him as if the pair of them were abroad on the breast of the ocean for the first time.

The key to survival was for the paddler to kneel comfortably on a bag of straw placed in the front of the currach, with the soles of his feet firmly wedged against a small block of wood fixed behind him to the bottom. Thus transfixed, there was less possibility of the paddler being pitched headlong into the sea by an unexpected wave movement. '*Coinnigh do bhonnaí leis an tac, coinnigh do bhonnaí leis an tac,*' roared Jack on his knees by the roadside in Tyrone, repeating his uncle's dire injunction to him to keep his feet tightly pressed against the life-saving support behind him.

While still a secondary schoolboy, I met numerous other Irish speakers from various parts of Donegal including Tory Island, Cloughaneely, Glenfinn, and Glenties, all of whom helped in one way or another to bolster my fledgling knowledge of Irish and its various dialects. The speech of a Cloughaneely woman – the mother of the man who married my mother's sister, Susie – was peppered with the negative particles *cha*, *chan*, and *char* which baffled my poor brain already hard put to grapple with the more commonplace forms of *ní* and their usages.

Eventually, my knowledge increased to the point where I was able to conduct a sensible conversation with those who were willing to talk. Some, however, viewed their knowledge of Irish as a badge of shame and saw my forcing my company on them as an unwelcome reminder of their origins and the reason that compelled them to leave home in the first place in search of a living among strangers. This process taught me many lessons, not all of them to do with grammar and vocabulary.

Once, one of my contacts became unwittingly embroiled in my schooling at the Christian Brothers Grammar School in Omagh when, in answer to my call, she supplied the Irish word for 'chicken' which featured in some simple homework exercise or other. I duly recorded the word *'eireog'* – which is, indeed, a word for 'chicken' or, more precisely, a pullet or one-year old hen. My passing over the expected *'sicín'* in favour of this somewhat technical alternative caused raised eyebrows, but otherwise occasioned no retribution from the teacher who may have been as perplexed by *'eireog'* as I had been myself.

Much to the delight of an aged neighbour called Frank Quinn who ran a small grocery store, I would often be sent to fetch a copy of the *Irish Press*, a paper we took daily, together with the *Irish News*. Frank, who was an ardent Republican of the anti-Treaty variety, loved Irish which he had learned as a prisoner on the prison ship *Argenta* on which he had been interned in Belfast Lough in the 1920s. He never missed the opportunity to exchange a few words in Irish with me, especially in the hearing of other customers.

A consequence of his political engagement was manifested one day in the early 1950s during a trip to Dublin when Frank, my father, and I were passing by what I now know were Government Offices on Merrion Street. All of a sudden, Frank stood rooted to the spot as a limousine began to emerge on to the street. Then, ramrod straight by the kerbside, he produced a crisp military salute which was returned with a friendly wave from a gaunt, bespectacled figure seated in the back. This, I was informed, was no less a personage than the Taoiseach of the day, Éamon de Valera, of whom, with my Northern upbringing, I knew precious little. From that episode, however, I learned that loyalty to 'The Chief' was alive and well in Langfield, at least as far as Frank Quinn was concerned, and I saw a completely new side to my neighbour, the quiet-spoken country shopkeeper with a past.

That my schooling should have fuelled rather than quenched my interest in Irish is down to two individuals – Larry Leather and Brother Thomas Nagle, whom we called 'The Bear'. The latter also carried a strap but, in my experience, rarely matched his other colleagues in ferocity. No doubt, he would have known and fully subscribed to the old Irish proverb triad – *'Trí rud gan feidhm; máistir scoile gan slat, píobaire gan dos, táilliúir gan méaracán'* – 'Three useless things: a schoolmaster without a rod, a piper without a drone, a tailor without a thimble.'

For all that he was a Munster man, born and bred, he was the author of our *vade mecum* – the Christian Brothers' Irish Grammar (*Graiméar na Gaedhilge* – Ulster version). Therein, forms typical of Donegal Irish were set out together with examples. The section on numerals explained the method of counting in which, unlike other dialects, Ulster Irish eschewed the distinction between the processes of counting people and counting things. Thus, *beirt, triúr* etc., normally 'two, three people', could also mean 'two or three things or objects'. The example given in Brother Nagle's grammar runs as follows: *'D'ól muid dhá ghloine uisce beatha agus d'ordaigh muid beirt eile!'* – 'We drank two glasses of whiskey and ordered two more!' This declaration would hardly be described as being politically correct by today's standards, nor would it have cheered the hearts of members of the Pioneer Total Abstinence Association, but it had the virtue of getting the message across quite succinctly.

Following my first couple of sojourns in the Gaeltacht, Brother Nagle spotted my enthusiasm for Irish and, on the eve of my impending return to Rannafast for another session, drew me aside and presented me with a long list of words which he had abstracted from the works of the Donegal writer, 'Máire' or Séamus Ó Grianna, a Rannafast native. Armed with this list I was to quiz Micí Sheáin Néill Ó Baoill (in whose house I would be billeted for the duration) as to the exact meaning of each item and to note down his comments. For all my tender years, I took this task seriously and, in a way, it led to my taking the first faltering steps in pursuit of the academic career that I would eventually follow.

Larry Leather also contributed to nurturing my academic interest in Irish. He had the advantage of teaching both Irish and English, and not only had a good knowledge of both languages, of course, but also a passion for dialects. To my astonishment, he enquired at one of our very first classes if any of us knew Irish. I remember marvelling that he should pose such a silly question, but he quickly showed that there was method in his madness by proceeding to fill the blackboard over and over with words familiar to us that we had blithely assumed were English, and with idioms and expressions with which we were all well acquainted and which we also took to be English.

The point was driven home that, whereas we had no real knowledge of Irish, at least we knew quite a few items of Irish vocabulary, and we also took on board that some of the complexities of Irish syntax were likely to be less of a mystery to us than we might have first imagined. He also pinpointed a range of phonetic features common to Irish and the kind of English we spoke, identifying with examples dental ts and ds, retroflex rs and ss, and broad and slender gs and cs, all of which came second nature to us, though of course we had no way of fathoming their significance as linguistic phenomena.

Fired by this knowledge, when making my first acquaintance with the verb *'Tá'*, I remember noting the various forms in my jotter followed by an approximation of their pronunciation as it sounded to me; after *'Tá siad'* – 'They are' – I wrote, 'shed', which we pronounced with a diphthong, making it sound not a million miles from the correct Irish pronunciation of *'siad'*.

So powerful was this epiphanic experience that I remember thinking that, with such a head start, learning Irish would be a cinch. Such was far from being the case, of course, but those revelations made a deep impression upon me and provided a psychological fillip that stood me in excellent stead afterwards. Today, asked by foreigners interested in Irish if Irish was my first language, I often think of the insights gained from that excellent teacher and sometimes go on to reply that, whereas I was not a native speaker of Irish, neither in any real sense was I a native speaker of the Queen's English, so suffused with substratum Irish words, idioms, syntax, and sounds was the dialect with which I grew up.

I liked writing English essays and Larry Leather was also responsible for spurring my interest in this aspect of the learning process. My mother encouraged me greatly in this respect, often reading and commenting upon my scribblings. I appeared in print at quite an early age, the forum being the children's section of the *Irish Press* edited by one 'Captain Mac'. My unsolicited offering in verse appeared in his column in the 25th March, 1952 edition of the paper and went as follows:

> I wake up in the morning to hear the Thrushes sing,
>   Upon the branches slender I see them hop and swing.
> I watch them flutter up and down waiting for the Worm.
> Their whistling cheers me up a lot early in the morn.

'Isn't that nice and happy and lively,' commented the good Captain, which is about as kind a comment as anyone could manage about this limp quatrain by a nine-year old boy.

Essay-writing was fraught with difficulty of an interesting nature, namely, the pervasive influence of my native dialect of English, shot through as it was by local words, expressions, and idioms, some of which had their roots in lowland Scots, but most of which stemmed from Irish. I well remember my bafflement at Larry Leather's rejection of such splendid lexical items as 'suvendable' (as in the phrase 'suvendably well' i.e. 'superb'), 'longsome' ('slow, tedious') and 'carnaptious' ('cranky')

– perfectly viable usage in my home environment, but red-pencil fodder in a school context.

In time, of course, I realized that the education system was not geared to cater for the likes of me. The key to future success lay in strictly conforming with expected norms, for such was the order of the day; inability to comply would ultimately result in failure and sometimes public ridicule along the way. The latter was precisely the fate that befell a pupil of Loreto Convent Grammar School in Omagh who, when her English teacher demanded a synonym for the verb 'to search', gaily piped up 'hoke, Miss!' instantly making a laughing stock of herself in the eyes of her fellow students.

It was a long time before I learned to cherish these and other colourful items from my stock of words and to cease struggling to find recognizable equivalents for them before banishing them for good. They were little use to me then, of course; now with the passage of time, I find it ever harder to recall them, never mind chance upon an occasion to deploy them in conversation. In my time there, everyday speech was laced with lexical items and modes of expression that lay outside normal parameters. When people paused to reflect upon them, these often proved to be a source of fascination and sometimes amusement. Mostly people fondly imagined anything out of the ordinary to be of Irish origin – almost wished for it to be so. Sometimes this was the case, but just as often such elements belonged to the Scots legacy. By and large, however, people did not differentiate or discriminate as to source between the twin streams of language that coalesced in colloquial parlance and informed everyday discourse.

At another level, however, such elements were often recognized as deviating from what would have been regarded as educated speech and, to a degree, people were conscious of that difference, some even self-conscious about it. Largely speaking, however, vocabulary was not a subject of debate, except for occasional advertence to particular usages, mostly in a spirit of fun. A point in question would be the word 'sheugh' in regard of which I often heard it said: 'How do you spell sheugh?' the answer to which was usually given as 'ess-haitch-ee-uch-uch', or the like. The word 'sheugh' (meaning a 'drain', or 'drainage channel') was sometimes associated with the word 'broo' (meaning a 'bank', or 'edge', from the Irish *bruach*) as in sayings such as 'out of the sheugh, onto the broo' i.e. 'out of the drain, onto the bank'.

More subtle and more tenacious by far are the many syntactical features and idiomatic expressions of my native dialect that have their origin in the Irish language. It has taken a lifetime for me to recognize a good many of them for what they are. Often it is the puzzled reaction of bamboozled acquaintances – signalling linguistic distress – that tips me off and sets me trying to hit upon a conventional English-language equivalent while searching my memory banks for the apposite Irish-language wording. I will not – nor, it seems, cannot – let go of these deep-seated features even though they have bedevilled my attempts to fully master the language in which I now seek to write. On the plus side, they have taught me a good deal about colour and nuance in language usage which might have otherwise eluded me.

I was well into my stride by the time I reached Fifth Class – 'O' (Ordinary) Senior Certificate Level – and sufficiently confident at that stage to enter an essay competition open to all the pupils of Omagh's various grammar schools, Catholic and Protestant. This competition was run by Omagh Rotary Club and featured a decent prize, a holiday abroad or something of that nature, as far as I recall.

The essay topic was 'Patriotism is Not Enough', a statement uttered by Edith Cavell, a heroic nurse executed by the Germans in World War I, though I knew nothing of the source of the quote or of Nurse Cavell at the time. To my astonishment (and to that of the school and my schoolmates, I sensed), I was one of three or four candidates short-listed, called to interview, and entertained to lunch by the Club. I felt hopelessly out of my depth and thoroughly intimidated by the surroundings. I performed badly and failed to get the nod, the prize going instead to an 'A'-level pupil of Omagh Academy, who was no doubt much more deserving of it.

Success of another kind was just around the corner, however, in the form of another competition, this time one organized by Gael Linn in grammar schools across the North. In this context, four two-month Gaeltacht scholarships were on offer, and a gold medal to boot for the outright winner. Still in Fifth Class, I came fourth in the competition, thus claiming a scholarship that once again brought me back to Rannafast in the summer of 1959. I entered again the following year, came first and was awarded the gold medal, but was docked 10% of the marks in order to facilitate the award of a scholarship to the individual who had gained fifth place and who would have not qualified otherwise. Though I felt a little miffed at the time, in retrospect it was a wise decision.

My interrogation on both occasions was led by Pádraig Ó Baoighill, himself a native of Rannafast and long-standing agent of Gael Linn and dedicated promoter of the Irish language in the North, where he was widely known as 'Paddy Gael Linn'. I believe it was at the second of these interviews that I was bowled the following googly, when he asked me to provide a translation of the phrase 'The crooked leg of the little black hen.' Somehow or other, I managed to render accurately the grammar-laden Irish version of this, viz. *'Cos cham na circe bige duibhe'*, and often wondered since if it was this that tipped the scales in my favour when it came to the gold medal award. I subsequently received from Paddy my very first hand-written letter in Irish in which I encountered a phrase new to me – *'maidir le'* ('as regards') – which sent me scurrying to the dictionary, proving, I suppose, that I still had a lot to learn.

My last year at the CBS Grammar School found me taking three subjects for the A-Level examinations, success in which would lead to university. At that time – presumably because of lack of resources – options at A-level were rather limited at the school and some of my favourite subjects such as History, Geography, or English, were unavailable to me. As a consequence I was forced to take Chemistry – a subject for which I had little interest and even less talent – and in unlikely partnership with Irish and Latin to make up the necessary trio, a combination in which I needed to gain an average of 40% for admission to QUB and, more significantly, an average of 50% to qualify for a university scholarship from Tyrone Education Authority, without the benefit of which there would be no chance of a university career for me. Others faced with the same dilemma, but generally more savvy than I or my parents, and blessed with the necessary financial wherewithal, solved the problem by taking subjects privately.

My labours at Latin produced a decent mark in the middle 60%s, but my half-hearted attempt at Chemistry turned in a result in the middle 30%s, barely qualifying for compensation. The morning of one of my Chemistry papers found me not in the examination hall but sound asleep in bed instead. A frantic phone call from the school principal and a mad dash by car to Omagh saw me take up my pen an hour or so into the examination. Not that it made a great deal of difference, for I had already succeeded in making a complete hames of the practical examination by blowing up my apparatus no less than three times in the course of an experiment I was required to conduct.

Irish saved the day for me, however, in that I received a mark of 94%, which was the highest mark achieved in A-Level Irish that year, thus sailing comfortably over the 50% bar, and setting a course for Belfast where I was to spend the greater part of the 1960s. Some of my classmates narrowly failed to make the cut and were compelled to endure another year at school in order to boost their average to the desired level. Ironically, the average of 50% in three subjects to gain a scholarship was suddenly reduced to 40% the following year.

IV

The 'No English' Rule

I HAD FIRST VISITED the Donegal Gaeltacht as an infant ensconced in a specially commissioned wickerwork basket laid on the back seat of the family car. My mother spoke of her travels with my father as far as Bloody Foreland, but I remember nothing of that. She also recalled meeting Irish speakers here and there and conversations with them, conducted, perforce, in English.

Following completion of my second year at the Christian Brothers Grammar School in Omagh, I spent July of that summer at *Coláiste Bhríde, Rann na Feirste*. My parents funded my sojourn in 'Rannafast', which was probably the only Irish college known to them. I had the good fortune to be billeted in the house known as *Teach Mhicí Sheáin Néill* inhabited at that time by Micí Sheáin Néill Ó Baoill, his sister Annie and her daughter Bríd, and, in later years, his brother John.

At the time, I was unaware of the circumstances that brought me to their door in the first place, blithely assuming (insofar as I understood anything about College procedures) that I just happened to have been allocated a place under their roof. How this came about may be worth rehearsing as a small illustration of the exercise of power and privilege in society, the like of which Northerners like myself had little opportunity to experience.

A classmate of mine in Omagh lived in Lifford, County Donegal, where his father was a high-level functionary within the county council bureaucracy. That he received his secondary education in Omagh was due (at least in part) to his being able to avail of the rail connection between Strabane and Omagh, courtesy of the Great Northern Railway (before Stormont did away with it).

He and his younger brother and I had been enrolled for

the course at *Coláiste Bhríde* and it was arranged that we would travel there together. Our driver – a county council colleague of my friend's father – duly deposited us at the College where after some short delay all three of us were installed in *Teach Mhicí Sheáin Néill*.

It soon became clear that three other lads already in residence had been removed elsewhere in order that the newcomers could be accommodated in what was clearly regarded as one of the top billets, being centrally situated and boasting a storyteller in residence. It seemed that this may have been the result of some high-powered intervention or other, of which I was the unwitting beneficiary. At any rate, the disgruntled evicted trio were clearly of that opinion and we were left in no doubt as to what they thought of the entire process and our part in it.

This infelicitous start to my first stay in Rannafast was followed by a period of enforced reticence in light of the 'No English' rule to which all students had signed up. In my case, this amounted to a vow of silence as my understanding of Irish was minimal and my knowledge of spoken Irish correspondingly poor. It was galling for me and other Northern students of my own age to be lodged in classrooms cheek by jowl with children of nine and ten whose schooling in Dundalk and other places south of the border had equipped them with what appeared to us to be dazzling fluency in the language but which in many cases was just fluent bad Irish, though I did not realize that at the time.

We talked some English *sotto voce* among ourselves, of course, always guarding against being overheard by a zealous minion of the College and suffering the indignity of being packed off home – *'ar an chéad bhus ar maidin'* – by the next bus. The teachers patrolled the roads, lanes, and pathways of Rannafast by night, lurking behind hedges and, in some cases, listening at bedroom casements, hoping to catch unwary transgressors of the language rule.

My parents came to visit and drove me around the district one afternoon. 'What's wrong with you, cub?' my mother asked at one point, having taken on board that I had hardly spoken two words for the duration of the excursion. So strong was the fear of expulsion that I had simply got out of the habit of talking at all. 'Cub' was the normal word for 'boy' just as 'cuttie' was the word for a girl.

The teachers at *Coláiste Bhríde* were a motley crew – some disciplinarian like Aodh Mac Eoin (a Belfast man nicknamed for some reason 'Fish and Chips'), others like Peadar Ó Ceallaigh from County Meath who rejoiced in nocturnal loitering in search of breachers of the 'No English' language code. We were taught to sing the old Donegal Gaeltacht songs by a master of the art – Aodh Ó Duibheannaigh – Hiúdaí Phaddy Hiúdaí – (or 'Oody Oo' as we disrespectfully pronounced it).

But by the 1950s, change was afoot even in that far-flung corner of Donegal. The lively traffic back and forward to Scotland in search of work, and the influx of visitors in July during what was known as 'The Glasgow Fair' brought new fashions and singing styles including those adopted by 'Teddy Boys'. Speaking English was strictly forbidden as far as we were concerned, but no such sanction applied to the (grand) sons of Rannafast who sometimes assembled of an evening in the shelter of the small building in which Hiúdaí Phaddy Hiúdaí taught us his songs during the day. I remember one young fellow who revealed a good tongue of Irish and a strong Scottish accent when strumming his guitar and giving vent to Rock 'n' Roll numbers of the day. He was surrounded by a circle of youthful Rannafast admirers who joined in the various numbers while we stood listening in silence.

Some learners of an older vintage also frequented those parts during the summer months in order to polish up their *'blas'*. They often tended to be militant about the use of English and were frequently aggressive about it. One such incident involved a number of them seeking directions from a man who lived on the fringe of Irish-speaking territory who when asked for help is said to have politely replied – 'I'm sorry, sir, but there's no Irish at me' (i.e. 'I have no Irish'). One of the visitors, incensed by this rebuff, is reported to have retorted – 'There's f... all English at you either!'

I heard Micí Sheáin tell of a gentler soul also engaged in the pursuit of Irish who had adopted his own personal 'No English' rule in an effort to amplify his very limited capacity in Irish. According to Micí this man also got lost, having gone astray on a wide stretch of bog somewhere in the vicinity. He wandered in circles until at last he came upon a solitary individual stacking turf to dry. Without delay, having

Micí Sheáin Néill

summoned up as much Irish as he could muster, the stranger addressed the local man saying *'Níl a fhios agam. An bhfuil a fhios agat?'* ('I don't know. Do you?'). The man on the bog understood his dilemma and indicated the location of the nearest road to him.

Rannafast was chock-a-block with noted storytellers and singers in those days, among them a man called Seán Bán Mac Grianna, a couple of whose brothers – Séamus and Seosamh – had made names for themselves in the field of Irish writing. We read their books for O-Level and A-Level examinations in Irish. Seán Bán was in receipt of the blind pension, being albino. He sported milk-bottle thick lenses in his glasses and often had difficulty in controlling the unruly students attending his classes in *Coláiste Bhríde*, especially since he could hardly see them.

One of these classes was held in a small lean-to affair attached to the College with just a few small windows to provide ventilation. It was there that the following incident occurred when one of the students (a fellow who subsequently joined an enclosed order) ordered the windows to be closed and then produced a small vial of ether, which he opened and placed on the rostrum beside the unfortunate Seán Bán who then proceeded to quietly drone himself to sleep. It was a cruel act to carry out on a helpless old man trying to do his best for us.

Seán Bán's brilliant command of Irish was the envy of all who knew anything about the language and the envy too of some who knew nothing. Once in a pub in nearby Annagry, Seán Bán was accosted by a boor who felt compelled to challenge his standing in this regard, 'You're supposed to know Irish,' said he, 'so tell me what's the Irish for myxomatosis?' Seán Bán flung the question back in his face by replying, 'You put English on it and I'll put Irish on it for you!' The word myxomatosis (used to describe an infectious and generally fatal disease among rabbits, prevalent in the 1950s) is ultimately of Greek origin.

We learned to grapple with all sorts of *céilí* dances, including the complex Sixteen Hand Reel and the High Cauled Cap, and in the process to engage with members of the opposite sex. Our teacher was a tiny Belfast man called Séamus Ó Mealláin, nicknamed 'Ducky' probably because he waddled like a duck. But he knew the dances for all that and put us through our paces relentlessly on a daily basis, sometimes *al fresco* on the tarred road outside the College. We also learned to smoke – in my case puffing Sweet Afton on the broad of my back in the heather, my head spinning so that I could not stand upright. At low tide on glorious summer Sundays, we waded across the *deán* (a narrow channel of sea-water) to frolic on the sands of Carrickfinn (or *An Pointe* as it was called) and later, like some straggling band of prisoners of war, made the long trek back via Mullaghduff and Annagry to Rannafast.

The requirement to provide accommodation and sustenance for six hundred schoolchildren was an enormous boost for the local economy. We slept three abed in many cases and survived on simple fare complemented by what edibles we could find and afford to buy in *Siopa Bhrianaí*, *Siopa Searcaigh*, or *Siopa Cassie*. The local hens were under considerable strain and eggs were in short supply, so much so that our weekly fry on a Sunday morning generally consisted of a single rasher and sausage accompanied by half a fried egg.

As my ability to understand and speak Irish increased, and something approaching normal conversation began to become possible, so Mící Sheáin's interest in me also seemed to blossom. Once we set off together from Rannafast, heading across the *deán* to *An Pointe*, or more specifically to a cluster of small thatched houses where a group of people known as *Albanaigh an Phointe* ('The Protestants of Carrickfinn') resided. Our mission was to buy as many eggs as we could carry and I was there to ease Mící's burden in transporting them back to Rannafast.

Along the way, I received a language lesson I will never forget as Mící maintained a constant commentary upon features of the landscape, identified flora and fauna, and showed me how to read the signs of life along the shore and beneath the sand. We drank of the water at the well spilling onto the strand and, as we approached our destination, Mící explained that while many of the *Albanaigh* spoke Irish we might happen on some who did not. In the event that I was spoken to in English I had from him a formal dispensation from the No English Rule to reply in that language. I learned that it was better to be civil than to cleave to any language diktat.

From Mící, I also heard for the first time of another language stronghold in central Donegal, namely *Na Cruacha* or The Croaghs. Glenfinn Irish-speakers were wont to praise Croaghs Irish for its purity – '*Tá seanGhaeilg mhaith fá na Cruacha!*' – 'There's real old Irish in the Croaghs!' they would say. Many years later, I travelled there with Mící and met up with some of the old-timers who were so impressed with his command of language that subsequently they always referred to him as '*an fear a bhfuil an Ghaeilg aige*' – 'the man who knows Irish'. He was deemed, in other words, to be as good as themselves. High praise indeed!

V

Mind Your Slender 'R's

THE NEXT STAGE in my education saw me take up residence in Belfast as a first-year student at Queen's University in the autumn of 1960. With a mixture of excitement and trepidation, I joined the throng of freshers launching into their new careers, many of them like myself from rural backgrounds, unaccustomed to city life and destined to live away from home for the first time. I was the first of my extended family to have the opportunity of getting a university education and one of the very few from my native parish to have progressed that far. Green and all as I was, I did not succumb to the temptations of city life as readily as another Omagh CBS boy a few years older than I. He, it was said, spent his first week at Queen's in the nearby Ulster Museum, not out of any all-consuming interest in history, archaeology, or art, but rather for the kick he got out of travelling up and down in the lift, for free.

The 1947 Education Act had opened the way for many of us, and the influx of students from a similar background to mine turned into a flood as time went on. I remember hearing that Catholics formed 25% of the Queen's student population at the time, a somewhat alarming statistic from my point of view as I had grown up in an overwhelmingly Catholic community and suddenly found myself cast in the role of a member of the minority. Headcounts like that were – and, unfortunately, still are – par for the course in the North.

One of my first duties as a first-year student was to see my Adviser of Studies, a lecturer in the English Department called John Braidwood. The attitude of this decent Scot to my declared intention of taking Irish (or Celtic as it was called) and Latin as two of my first-year subjects was a revelation to me and a real tonic – 'An excellent combination,' he declared.

Scholastic Philosophy was recommended as a possible third subject – a kind of filler. There was a Philosophy department at Queen's too, but mainstream Philosophy, open to all comers, was not recommended for Catholics, or so we were told.

It is likely to have been the Catholic Chaplain, Father Patrick Kelly, who was responsible for conveying that message to me during my mandatory consultation with him after I had arrived on campus. I do remember distinctly his outburst when I informed him of my having enrolled to do Celtic and he left me in no doubt as to the the uselessness of such a pursuit and the waste of opportunity it represented. Raw and all as I was, I knew enough to pay no heed to him and left with a feeling of disgust and disappointment, in sharp contrast to the lift that John Braidwood's words of encouragement had earlier given me. I suppose, to be fair to Father Kelly, he may have seen it as his job to push young Catholics in the direction of gaining professional qualifications of one kind or another in order that they might better themselves and assist in improving the lot of Catholic people generally. But his dismissal of me and my interest in Irish rankled at the time and still does to this day.

In any case, I had little choice but to stick with Scholastic Philosophy, which I abandoned at the end of first year to concentrate on Celtic, with Latin as my second-year subsidiary subject. I then went on to complete my four-year degree course in Celtic Studies, graduating in the summer of 1964.

Two of my teachers in Scholastic Philosophy were Theodore Crowley OFM and Father James Mackey. A third cleric, though one with whom I had no connection, was Father Cathal Daly, later to become Cardinal Archbishop of Armagh. Theodore Crowley was an imposing figure of a man and worldly wise to match. James Mackey with his film-star looks was the darling of the women, some of whom were so besotted as to write blackboard love messages to him.

Theodore Crowley was fond of regaling us with stories of his travels around the world. Once he told of a visit to the Congo where in sweltering heat he was making his way from the airport to the capital by taxi. In a lather of sweat, he asked the driver to open first one window and then, shortly after, a second. With great bad grace the driver obliged by opening one window, but when requested to open a second, he immediately pulled up, got out of the car and, before resuming his journey, donned a heavy overcoat which he had in the boot. I forget entirely the point of this story which may have been quoted in order to drive home some finer point of philosophical reasoning. The point eludes me now (and perhaps also then), but I remember the story.

In my undergraduate days at Queen's I lodged in a variety of digs scattered around the perimeter of the campus, most of which were cheap and of uniformly poor quality. It was an entirely different matter when I made the move to 26 Camden Street and the home of a kindly couple called Patrick and Bridget Kelly. For me and the other lodgers, this was a home away from home. The welcome was warm and the weekly stipend reasonable. My stay there extended into postgraduate years and the friendship between me and Pat (from Crossgar in County Down) and Bridget (from Brookeborough in County Fermanagh) never waned. They have now gone to their reward, God be good to them.

I have to admit that I was not a particularly industrious student, though I did attend most of my lectures and tutorials and was a regular visitor to the university library. I was drawn to one of the first books I discovered there by its title – *A Dialect of Donegal* – E.C. Quiggin's classic study of the Irish of Meenawannia, a townland a few miles south of the town of Glenties, but found its contents altogether too technical for my comprehension at that stage.

Like other second-year Honours students, I was granted privileged access to what were called 'the stacks' – i.e. the upper levels of the library on which the library holdings were shelved and

OLD LIBRARY AT QUEEN'S

stored. There I found more books about Ireland and matters Irish than I ever imagined to exist. Among them were numerous volumes of the Henry Collection, named after a patriotic Irishman and former Professor of Latin at Queen's, and others bearing the signature of T. F. Ó Rathaile, a leading Dublin scholar whose books had been snapped up by the university from bookshops along the Quays in Dublin, it was said. Slender financial resources permitted few book purchases, but Serridge's bookshop in Castle Street, where one could occasionally find a bargain, was always a draw for all that. I remember purchasing past numbers of *Béaloideas* there for as little as sixpence or a shilling.

The teaching was led throughout by Heinrich Hans Wagner (1923-1988), the Professor of Celtic, who exercised an enormous influence on my life as a student. He was a Swiss linguist and scholar, and an exotic figure because of his strange Swiss-German accent in English combined with impeccable Donegal Irish. He was at various stages aided and abetted across a range of subjects such as Old Irish, Scottish Gaelic, Welsh, Classical Irish, Irish dialects, *Fiannaíocht*, and Folklore by others, both permanent and transient members of staff. These including a young Corkonian by the name of Breandán Ó Buachalla (later Professor of Modern Irish at University College Dublin), a Belfast woman by the name of Deirdre Morton (later Flanagan) who dazzled us with her superb command of Donegal Irish (not to mention her good looks!), Patrick Leo ('P.L.') Henry from North Roscommon, whose forbidding exterior and gruff manner concealed a heart of gold, and his wife, Siobhán, from *Corca Dhuibhne* in Kerry, who read Munster Irish texts with us. Colm Ó Baoill from Armagh and Gearóid Stockman from Belfast, Dick Skerritt from Dublin, Anraí Mac Giolla Chomhghaill and Nollaig Ó hUrmoltaigh from Derry were also involved with us in various ways at various junctures, while Seán Ó hEochaidh from Donegal and James Carney from the Dublin Institute for Advanced Studies also made intermittent appearances in our midst. Among our Welsh teachers were Bruce Williams (formally of Queen's Department of French) and Mrs Williams, a Welshwoman living in exile in Belfast. Our one-year course in Celtic Archaeology was conducted by Professor E.M. Jope of the Archaeology Department at Queen's.

Just before the Christmas break in first year, I and several other students were singled out by Paddy Henry and charged with preparing a précis of a chapter in Daniel Corkery's *The Hidden Ireland*. I had no idea what was meant by a précis and being too shy to ask was compelled to resort to a dictionary for further elucidation. Being the rather too literal fellow that I am at times, I spent that Christmas at home in Drumquin, honing and paring, cropping and compressing Corkery's literary musings to beat the band, eventually fetching up with as tight a package as anyone could possibly have achieved. I turned in my work with pride on my return to Belfast, confident that the half page I had struggled so mightily to produce would meet the bill and be viewed with approbation. Paddy soon punctured my expectations as he raised my précis aloft and harrumphed, 'It's a bit on the short side, isn't it!' I was bemused – after all wasn't that what a précis was supposed to be? I did not see the fun of it at the time, but in its own curious way, it proved to be a valuable lesson. My well-honed half page was dismissed as unacceptable. So much for dictionary definitions. One lives and learns.

Heinrich's English pronunciation sometimes became the object of cruel mimicry, as illustrated by a comment he was said to have made in the course of his critique of a certain female student's rendition of an Irish text which he had asked her to read aloud for him. Her particular difficulty centred on rendering a clear distinction between the broad and slender varieties of the consonant 'r', a matter of considerable moment in good spoken Irish. 'Ach vell Miss X,' Heinrich is said to have innocently intoned in gentle reprobation, 'you must mind your slender *r*s'!

The Gaelic Society /*An Cumann Gaelach* was the first of a small number of societies I had joined on arrival at Queen's and I remained a member for all my days there. I served as a committee member and editor of *An Scáthán*, its modest magazine – in reality a cyclostyled production amateurishly typed up my myself and other equally inexperienced students – and was also elected *Leas-Reachtaire* of the Society in due course.

QUEEN'S UNIVERSITY BELFAST

During one of the early Queen's Festivals we pulled off what we regarded as something of a coup in securing an interview (in Irish) with Mícheál Mac Liammóir who received us with his customary flair in the Wellington Park Hotel on the Malone Road. Much to our astonishment, another star turn at the Festival that year overheard us speaking Irish and took time out from his high stool at the bar to roundly abuse us for indulging in such foolishness. It turned out to be the only encounter I ever had with the Listowel playwright, John B. Keane.

The Gaelic Society organized *céilís* at various venues including Rag Week *Céilís* in the George VI Hall (near City Hall), the Ard-Scoil in Divis Street and St Mary's Hall on the Falls Road, all of which were well attended. Other more modest events took place at the likes of the newly built Methodist Centre near Queen's where we were made most welcome by the Reverend Ray Davey, the ecumenical cleric later closely associated with the Corrymeela Centre in north

Antrim. One out-of-town *céilí* sticks in my memory, not for the trek there and back or the evening's manoeuvres, but for the venue, which was Delargy's Hotel in the village of Cushendall in the Glens of Antrim. As I learned many years after, it was the ancestral home of James Hamilton Delargy /Séamus Ó Duilearga. It is no longer standing having been, as the great man himself used to put it, 'blown up by the patriots.'

For all that, *An Cumann Gaelach* tended to be viewed as a republican redoubt and hotbed of sedition. For many, it seemed, taking an active interest in the old tongue and its associated culture was tantamount to constituting a threat to the Six-County entity. To the best of my knowledge, no such connections political or otherwise existed or found expression in any of its activities.

On the other hand, one of the great benefits of the Society in those days was its links with an organisation called *An Comhchaidreamh*, an intervarsity grouping that facilitated cultural gatherings and debates at all the universities on the island and in various Gaeltacht venues such as *Gaoth Dobhair* in County Donegal and *An Fheothanach* in *Corca Dhuibhne*, County Kerry. *An Comhchaidreamh* was the brainchild of Gael Linn and its operation opened a window for many of us – including myself – on another world of which we knew precious little, and enabled us to form friendships with like-minded students from every corner of Ireland.

The highlight of the year for us was the Society's annual formal Dinner and *Céilí* where, in best bib and tucker, we celebrated our Irishness in the McMordie Hall at Queen's or in the more salubrious surroundings of the Wellington Park Hotel. These activities provided opportunities for practising our spoken Irish not to mention the conduct of fleeting romantic encounters.

My university scholarship was paid by Tyrone County Council in two moieties issued by cheque at the beginning of the first and second terms. The second payment, amounting to £108, was the larger of the two. I led a fairly frugal existence and so had managed to survive through the spring of 1962 on what remained of the September stipend. I was looking forward to blowing my savings in the Donegal Gaeltacht in due course. Shortly after the summer examinations, I arrived back in Drumquin proudly waving my cheque for all to see. My euphoria lasted less than 24 hours, for the very next day my father asked me for the money in order to settle a long overdue bill from the firm that supplied him with coffins and associated paraphernalia. I understood the seriousness of the situation and handed over the cheque without hesitation, wrecking my plans for gallivanting in the Gaeltacht that summer. The money emanated from the same County Council that had succeeded in putting my father out of business, so in a sense, there was an element of poetic justice to the whole affair. Small consolation.

In July 1963, I made my way for the first time to the mountain fastnesses of south-central Donegal. My path led me to the upper reaches of the Reelan River that rushes down to join the Finn as it flows north-eastwards to meet the Mourne at Strabane and Lifford, where it becomes the Foyle and reaches down to the sea at Derry. Buried among the hills where the Reelan rises is a cluster of townlands, spread along the sides of a deep river valley where three parishes meet – Kilteevoge, Inishkeel, and Killymard.

The names of many of these townlands contain the element *cruach* ('mountain stack') in reference to the precipitous slopes towering on either side of the infant Reelan as it tumbles down between them. Rising majestically on either side are colour-coded *An Dearg-Chruach* (The Red Stack) and *An Dubh-Chruach* (The Black Stack), as well as *An Leath-Chruach* (The Half-Stack), the euphonically titled *Cruach Mhín an Fheannta* (The Smooth Stack of the Flaying Wind) and shiny *Cruach an Airgid* (The Silver Stack) sometimes dubbed *'An baile is deise ainm in Éirinn'* ('The most pleasantly named townland in Ireland').

Presiding over these and adjacent peaks is *An Chruach Ghorm* itself, the only one not to have a townland named after it; instead, its anglicized form – 'The Blue Stack' – has been subsumed into the name of the entire range ('The

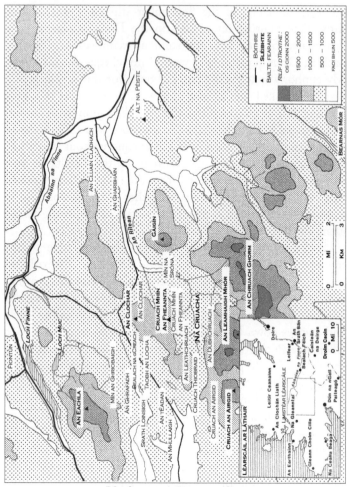

'NA CRUACHA', DÚN NA NGALL

Blue Stack Mountains'). Irish speakers know the area as 'Na Cruacha', generally rendered 'The Croaghs' in local English. These peaks were visible from the high ground in Langfield, whence the journey there by car took less than an hour.

That summer of 1963, scholarships from *Comhaltas Uladh* – the Ulster branch of *Conradh na Gaeilge* or Gaelic League (through the good offices of its then secretary, a decent man called Gearóid Mac Giolla Domhnaigh) – enabled a small

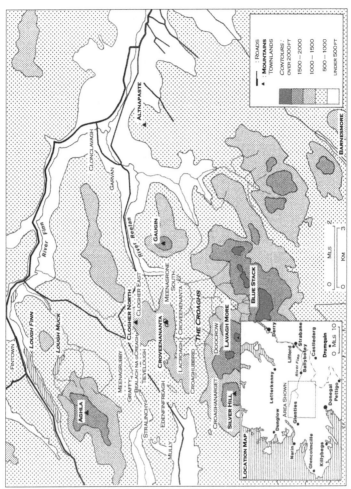

'The Croaghs' of Co. Donegal

group of budding Irish speakers, including myself, to sojourn in *Na Cruacha*. One of these was an old school friend and university companion in arms, Peadar Ó Duibheannaigh, from Omagh. Also part of this select group were two clerical students, one of whom went on to become a bishop.

We were billeted in the local houses and attended daily classes in the local primary school under the tutelage of its headmistress and only teacher, Máire Bean Uí Cheallaigh or

Mary Amrais as she was known locally. This bright, intelligent woman and local patriot spared no effort in sharing her knowledge of the dialect with us and all of us benefited greatly from the opportunity to learn. It was during this stay that I met, for the one and only time, a famous member of the musical Doherty family, the fiddler known as Mickey Simie and his wife Mary Rua. Mickey and Mary stayed with Fanny McGinley, a voluble, roly-poly figure who loved company and music. That day Mící played all manner of tunes by the open hearthside including an air that caught my attention. In answer to my question, he replied that it was called 'Going to Mass Last Sunday'. Various members of the Doherty family would spend longer spells living in households (months at a time in some cases) in different parts of Donegal such as *Na Cruacha*, moving out at intervals from their home base which in later years was located in the town of Stranorlar. I would later meet with Mickey's brother, John, who was extended the right hand of friendship in similar manner in the home of Pat Eoghain Mhícheáil and his household.

Summer jobs were a feature of student life at Queen's as elsewhere. Following the summer examinations, gangs of students would head for England, many to Kent to work on the buses, and others to factories producing peas and other vegetables. My first experience of a summer job was in Portadown, County Armagh. That was just before I went up to Queen's while I was waiting for my A-level results. My mother's sister, Margaret, and her husband Tommy Fullan lived there, and we as children had often been shipped off to stay with them for our 'holidays'. They were fond of us and of other nephews and nieces as they had no children of their own, apart from two phantom figures called James and Catherine whom we never met because they were forever away 'at boarding school', but in fact they did not exist.

Portadown was and still is one of the most sectarian places in the North and, while carefully cosseted by Tommy and Margaret from contact with the worst of that kind of thing, we were well aware that the situation there was not quite as easygoing as at home in Langfield. The Pleasure Gardens across

the road from us in Bridge Street by the River Bann with
its swings and roundabouts and carefully manicured bowling
greens was a great delight except on Sundays when, while the
gate remained open, we found the facilities within padlocked
and chained in order, presumably, to assist us in keeping holy
the Sabbath Day. I remember playing Cowboys and Indians
one day with a group of lads my own age in the nearby Public
Park when, suddenly, I found myself under interrogation as to
whether or not I was 'a Papish'. I was unable to answer this
question for the simple reason that I did not understand what
they were talking about. My silence was sufficient to reveal all
and that was the end of our childish games together.

I did not last long at my first job in Portadown which
was in the famous rose gardens of Sam McGready. Here I
was to spend my time picking thorns from the stems of rose
bushes, a task that left the fingers bleeding and sore, and all
for a measly few pounds a week. I threw in the towel after
a few days, but fortunately another more congenial position
was found for me almost immediately as a trainee barman
in the Imperial Hotel in the centre of the town. With the
help of the benevolent owner and her kindly staff members I
soon became adept at the work. At the end of summer, I was
approached by the owner who, having formed the opinion that
I was a likely lad, generously offered to fund my education in
hotel management, should I choose to follow that career.

The behaviour of one of the regular customers – a
retired schoolmaster – was also instrumental in educating
me in another way. This individual persisted in inviting me
to join him for afternoon tea at his home on my days off.
I instinctively knew there was something amiss and I had
no intention of yielding to his entreaties, fending him off as
politely as I could. One such encounter was overheard by the
hard-bitten (ex British Army) hotel chef who, believing me to
be in danger, took me to one side as I was passing through the
kitchen to advise me that if I accepted your man's invitation
I'd better be wearing iron drawers, as he put it. Enough said!

While still at Queen's, the following summer I got another
bar job this time in a far western suburb of Glasgow called

Yoker, hard by the shipyards in Clydebank. The Forum Bar was a vast establishment catering mainly for the thirst of shipyard workers and, at weekends, their wives and sweethearts. It was owned by a tough Cavan man who paid me £11 a week and worked myself and the other staff hard. I lodged gratis with old friends of my father and mother – John and Sadie Hamilton. At the end of the summer, I spent most of my savings on a train and boat trip via Oban to the Outer Isles to spend some time in Barra in an attempt to come to terms with Scottish Gaelic. There I had the good fortune to meet with a famous singer and promoter of Gaelic culture, a local schoolmistress called Annie Johnstone. Her first question to me was to enquire if I knew Séamus Ó Duilearga. In time, I came to know this man and his life's work more intimately than I could have then imagined.

What free time I had in Glasgow, I often spent in the company of a man called Tommy Docherty, who worked in some sort of sales or managerial capacity with Dunns, one of the largest mineral water and soft drinks firms in the city and one of the few Catholic firms of consequence there at that time. On his rounds, Tommy would take me to pubs and premises owned or managed by Highlanders who had the Gaelic, with whom I would attempt to engage. Once he arranged with the owner of Dunns to entertain me to dinner at the latter's home in Bearsden, a plush Glasgow suburb. There were just the three of us, Tommy, myself, and the old man who ran the show. I believe the object of the exercise may have been for me to be assessed with a view to future employment with the firm, in what capacity I cannot say. My memories of the occasion are hazy, however, and in any case I heard no more about it. Perhaps, all too jejune to comprehend what was going on, I may have made it all too clear that I fancied Celtic Studies a good deal more than a career in bottling.

My next foray into the bar trade the following summer was short-lived. It brought me to the Isle of Man and a hotel bar at the northern extremity of Douglas. There, in the Texas Bar, clad in bolero, chaps, and stetson, with a holster and toy pistol on my hip, I served drinks to drunken tourists (mostly from

Belfast). A typical order would be: 'Thee Mackies by the nack Jum!' – which meant 'Three Mackeson (stout) in an opened bottle, Jim! At the end of one week, I quit, checking in my outfit and heading back to Ireland. That was the ignominious end of my international career in the vintners' trade. Not long after I heard to my great satisfaction that the pint-sized tyrant who was my boss in Douglas was caught with his hand in the till and forced to depart the scene under a cloud.

In my final undergraduate year at Queen's, I knuckled down but should have done more work in Old Irish. Present at the oral were Heinrich Wagner, Paddy Henry (later Professor of Old and Middle English at UCG), and another UCG man – Tomás Ó Máille – the extern examiner and professor of Modern Irish in Galway. In the course of this grilling I was handed a facsimile page from the *Book of Leinster* – a medieval Irish manuscript compiled in 1160 AD – and asked to read and translate a marked passage, sight unseen. At one glance, I saw that I could manage to expand the manuscript contractions it contained and I also realized that I could translate the first of its two sentences, while knowing that the second was completely beyond me. I read the passage aloud and then

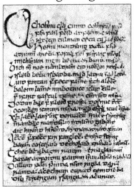

BOOK OF LEINSTER

proceeded to translate with conviction as far as I could. Happily, just before I would have been forced to bring matters to a halt and admit defeat, Paddy Henry signalled that I had done enough and I was spared further travail.

The result guaranteed me a Northern Ireland Ministry of Education postgraduate scholarship, enabling me to enrol for the Master of Arts degree by thesis. My supervisor was Heinrich Wagner. In the autumn of 1964, I would begin my apprenticeship in the world of scholarship, with £600 a year over two years to sustain me, a mighty handsome sum in those days.

VI

In Pursuit of Irish
Ar Thóir na Gaeilge

M Y THESIS was to be based on a placename study of two parishes in central Donegal – Kilteevoge and Inishkeel (or Glenfinn and Glenties to give them their popular names), for which purpose I needed wheels. So, with my father's expert guidance, I became the proud owner of an old Ford Anglia (upright model) that set me back the princely sum of £20. Not long after I upgraded to a Ford Prefect (also an upright model) that cost me twice the price and rendered faithful service for many years.

Apart from suffering minor mechanical failures of one kind or another from time to time, it ran well except for an overenthusiastic dynamo which tended to pump excessive power into the battery. In order to guarantee the latter's continued well-being I was compelled to drive around day and night with all lights blazing, barely stopping short of constantly blowing the horn and manically signalling with the bright orange indicators that stuck out on either side of the front doors as a way of further reducing the input charge that might blow up my battery.

The Prefect's roomy interior and fancy running boards outside compensated somewhat for these inconveniences, but a hole in the floor just behind the driver's seat meant that exhaust fumes threatened to poison the atmosphere within, and I was frequently forced to steer a course with my neck craned at an angle towards the quarter light in order to breathe. In addition, the heater only functioned spasmodically so that in winter I generally drove around with my feet and legs swathed in a rug. My awkward posture must have drawn some strange looks and, in truth, I was probably a danger to myself and other road-users, but luckily no damage was done to me or anyone else. Years later I sold the Prefect for half the price I paid for it and its new owner knocked good service out of it before it finally let him down on some garage forecourt where he promptly disposed of it for scrap.

I was briefed on the intricacies of onomastic research techniques by Deirdre Flanagan who had a strong interest in the subject and was closely connected with the Ulster Place-Name Society. She introduced me to a range of early sources – largely Plantation documents (Chancery Rolls and Inquisitions) specifying the granting of lands to various Undertakers and other agents of the Crown in the early decades of the seventeenth century. However outlandish these recorded anglicized versions of townland and other names were, they often provided useful reflections of the original Irish forms that facilitated their proper interpretation.

Heinrich's contribution largely consisted in ensuring that I was sufficiently au fait with phonetics as to be able to note down the names exactly as they were pronounced. In addition to the training in the art that I had received as an undergraduate, I was despatched into the field in the company of Annraoí Mac Giolla Comhghaill, then employed as Heinrich's Research Assistant. At various locations in Donegal, we were to supplement the materials already assembled for Wagner's monumental *Linguistic Atlas and Survey of Irish Dialects*.

My close acquaintance with the people of *Na Cruacha* had begun some years earlier, at the home of Pat and Rodie Gibbons and their son, Joe, in Dergroagh. My father had driven an undergraduate comrade-in-arms at Queen's, my brother Aidan, and me, together with our camping gear, across the border and up Glenfinn, heading for the hills. Pat's brother, Ned, who was the postmaster at *An Coimín*, near the Reelan bridge, piloted us to the Gibbons's homestead.

Pat gave us permission to pitch our tent at a little distance from the house and we set up camp while he and my father fell to talking about a friend they held in common, a Father Gormley, a much-admired priest whom my father knew from the time he had served in Langfield. Pat had also known him due to somewhat different circumstances, for he had been hired as a servant boy on the Gormley family farm in Glenmorning in the Sperrin Mountains. That was an Irish-speaking household which suited the young Donegal man well. He greatly enjoyed his time there and spoke warmly of the family and the people of the district. His experience was different from that of many other young Donegal boys and girls who often suffered great hardship and exploitation at the hands of cruel farmers.

Pat, Rodie, and Joe Gibbons were all excellent Irish speakers, but Pat, the man of the house, was the only one fully at home in English. I do not believe I heard Rodie utter a single word in that language even to my brother, Aidan, whose knowledge of Irish was fairly rudimentary. She took a great shine to him and with a fond smile would clasp his arm and say every time he crossed her path: *'Tá tú comh bog le héan gé'* – 'You're as soft as a gosling!' On subsequent visits to that household, she would welcome me back in old-world style, kissing my hand with little cries of delight. Aidan's minimal Irish and Joe's poor command of English led Joe to turning this situation to his advantage for, day in day out, he would eschew our company and draw Aidan aside, saying 'Come on Aidan, we'll speak the English the day!'

They enjoyed each other's company and Aidan still recalls the happy hours he spent with Joe, spotting salmon lurking in pools of the Reelan river, and helping Joe to 'herd' a suitable specimen into a tight corner where it could be speared with a harpoon which Joe called in Irish a *'morú'* or in English (or rather Scots) a *'leester'*. We ate well of one such fish which cost us an old, red Irish ten-shilling note. Cut into thick steaks and fried in butter at our campfire it lasted for days until we finally grew sick of it. I saw another hefty fish wrapped in nettles to keep it fresh for transport to another buyer elsewhere.

Pat was by far the best conversationalist of the three and full of anecdotes, some of them quite racy. I put him on the spot many a time because of my ignorance which had him searching for English translations or alternative descriptions to put me in the picture. A good example would be his casual remark to me: *'Tá an phlanóid athruithe, a Shéamais'* – 'The climate has changed, Séamas' – whereby I was introduced to an elegant word for 'climate' of an early vintage, one that owed nothing to modern-day book learning.

Typical of his style was the story he told of a young fellow who had tarried too long at the fair and faced a long and lonely walk home. He set off as evening came on and soon fell in with a pretty girl also stepping her way in the same direction. The weather turned foul as night fell and so they were forced to seek shelter until morning. They headed for a distant light and came to a house where they were allowed to take refuge from the storm, but denied the only free bed under that roof when asked, *'An lanúin sibh?'* – 'Are you married?'

They had to go further and once again spotted a light and came to another house. There they met a similar welcome and interrogation and once again were compelled to hit the road in what by now was a raging tempest of wind and rain. Thoroughly soaked, they reached yet another house and, as they approached the door, the young lady suggested to her male companion that things had gone quite far enough and that he might consider making a positive response to the inevitable enquiry as to their marital status.

He took her advice and, this time, he assured their hosts that they were indeed a couple and so they were duly granted access to the only free bed in the house. They were given something to eat and having dried themselves by the fire went to bed. As soon as they entered the chamber, the young fellow grabbed the bolster and drew it up the middle of the bed, dividing it into two sections, his and hers.

They slept sound until morning, ate their breakfast, paid the reckoning, and set off once more. The wind was still blowing a hurricane and a vicious gust swept the young lady's broad-brimmed hat from her head and blew it aloft. As it disappeared over a high bank by the roadside, the young fellow dashed in pursuit of the hat saying that it wouldn't take him long to retrieve it. 'Ha,' said she, 'there's little chance of your getting over that high bank today when you couldn't clear the bolster last night!'

Rodie had style and good manners. Her welcome was always a hearty torrent of words, accompanied by a hand clasp and a hand kiss, the old-world gesture now all but disappeared. Her welcome for members of the clergy was equally courteous but more formal, being notable especially for her deployment of the appropriate honorific form of salutation: *'Cad é mar tá sibh, a Athair?'* – 'How are you [plural] Father?'

During that short stay with Pat and Rodie, I got to know members of various local families – the Gibbonses, the Givens, the Wards, Quinns, Timoneys, Campbells, McHughs and, in particular, assorted McAloons. The latter constituted one of the largest groupings, some if its members being among the most talented storytellers and singers of the district, although the paterfamilias, Pádraig Eoghain Phádraig 'ac a' Luain, had a reputation for not suffering fools gladly. This trait was well-known to Seán Ó hEochaidh who, as a full-time collector with the Irish Folklore Commission, had garnered such a rich harvest in that district in the late 1940s. So overwhelmed was Seán by the abundance of folklore and talented informants available to him there that he felt little need for intensive engagement with Pádraig – or so he told me.

PÁDRAIG EOGHAIN PHÁDRAIG

I had been encouraged to seek out Pádraig and his siblings by Pat Gibbons and simultaneously warned about Padraig's fiery temperament. I had originally arrived sans tape recorder (for I did not possess such at the time) to a friendly, if bemused, reception from all three who wondered who the young stranger might be and what should bring him to their door. Somewhat miraculously in retrospect, Pádraig yielded to my importuning on that occasion, and recited a fragment of a tale of Fionn and the Fianna, while chewing on a hunk of home-made bread and supping a bowl of tea, before sending me packing and returning to his work in the fields.

Over the years, I was to become a regular visitor to that household, occasionally accompanied by my wife, sometimes with friends from elsewhere in Ireland or from abroad, and sometimes alone.

Like many

MAJ WITH MÁIRE & CONALL 'AC A' LUAIN

of their neighbours, Pádraig, his mild-mannered younger bachelor brother, Conall, and gentle sister Máire had an abiding interest in music and song, inherited in their case from their father, Eoghan Phádraig 'ac a' Luain, a noted singer of the locality. Eoghan Phádraig had been one of Seosamh Laoide's sources, having been summoned to rendezvous with this early twentieth-century intrepid, peripatetic collector in Donegal Town where they spent a pleasurable spell together. Eoghan Phádraig had trekked up and over the mountains and down by Loch Eske at the foot of their southern escarpment to get there, while Laoide (or 'Lide' [= 'Lloyd'] as Pádraig pronounced it with a thick velar 'l') arrived from Dublin, courtesy of the railway.

Eoghan Phádraig had passed away some forty years before I came on the scene, but was still very fondly remembered by his children who constantly reminisced about him and his songs. Once, in full voice at a Harvest Fair in Glenties, Eoghan Phádraig's singing was so much the centre of attraction that, as Conall put it, *'Ní bhfaighfeá do mhéar a chur ar an bhord'* ('You couldn't find room to place your finger on the counter'), for all the drinks that had been bought for him. On his return home from forays of this sort, Eoghan Phádraig might stand in the kitchen, back to the fire, and sing song after song, sometimes as many as three in a row.

To put it mildly, Eoghan Phádraig's song genes – or at least the singing voice element of them – failed to transfer to Pádraig or Conall or, as far as I know, to Máire, though all three were well versed in the various items making up their father's repertoire and could 'word' his songs perfectly. Pádraig would usually lead the way, the other two supplying lines and interpolating words should he falter. They did so at their peril for, as he concentrated on recalling the start of a particular verse and one or other of them might attempt to jog his memory, he was likely to snap: *'Níl gar don bheirt againn a dhul ann!'* – literally 'There's no need for both of us to go into it!' i.e. 'into' the tape recording.

Once, I played a recording of the famous Anna Nic a' Luain with whom Seán Ó hEochaidh had worked so intensively. She had a fine singing voice, but on the extant recordings of her, made on sixteen-inch discs by Caoimhín Ó Danachair on behalf of the Irish Folklore Commission, Anna 'words' rather than sings her songs, apart from the odd chorus here and there when she simply cannot help lapsing into song. Ó hÉochaidh told me that this was because Anna suffered from blood pressure and singing was far too stressful an exercise for her. The siblings listened intently to Anna's voice, once so familiar to them and, like the true connoisseurs they were, commented as one when she recited the final words: *'D'fhág sí ceathrú amháin amuigh!'* – 'She left out a verse!'

In similar vein, I heard from a local source of a famous evening of song and music in another McAloon household, *Teach Eoghain Mhicheáil*, into which Séamus Ennis, the renowned piper, had been introduced by Seán Ó hEochaidh. There was piping and fiddling and singing aplenty on that occasion. At some point in the proceedings, Ennis sang *Casadh an tSúgáin* to an audience packed to overflowing into the capacious kitchen of *Bunadh Eoghain Mhicheáil*. As the last note sounded and the cheers rang out, a voice from the back of the crowd was heard to say: *'Tá ceathrú eile ann!'* – 'There's another verse to it!' whereupon Pádraig

Eoghain Phádraig, who was tone deaf, triumphantly intoned the extra quatrain in his own inimitable atonal style.

Many years later, I heard him 'sing' the whole song when, together with a few friends, I happened upon him and Conall and Máire struggling late in the season to save a few cocks of hay. We raked and the three old-timers built and in no time at all, the job was complete whereupon a delighted Pádraig leaning on his hay-rake was inspired to deliver an *al fresco* version of *Casadh an tSúgáin*.

Pádraig Eoghain Phádraig lived with Conall and Máire in a long, low thatched house in *Cruach Mhín an Fheannta* (or Crooveenananta, as the name of this townland is grotesquely rendered on the Ordnance Survey maps of the district). Their dwelling offered little by way of home comforts, consisting of a kitchen and a room over which extended a half-loft facing towards the smoke hole at the gable wall, beside which was an outshot bed. Other kitchen furnishings consisted of a dresser, a couple of cupboards,

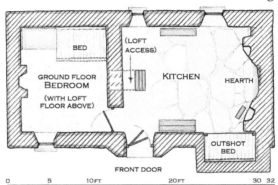

TYPICAL TWO-ROOM DONEGAL HOUSE WITH OUTSHOT, SIMILAR TO *TEACH EOGHAIN PHÁDRAIG* (BASED ON 1935 PLAN)

a few chairs, and a small collapsible triangular wooden table which was affixed to the back wall beside a small window opening, and was supported when folded down by a single leg under its outer edge. In pride of place, by the fireside opposite the outshot bed, was Pádraig's 'easy chair' – a disused car seat. The house was fully thatched when I first saw it but fell into decline with the passing years. Later, the roof had to be covered by an ugly black tarpaulin.

Like the old houses elsewhere (Langfield included) its thick stone walls held the heat well in winter and made for the maintenance of a cool interior in the heat of summer. The open half-door provided light and ventilation as well as functioning as a bulwark against marauding domestic fowl and dogs. Artificial light was supplied by a tall Aladdin oil-lamp and, later, a Tilley lamp, just as was the case in Granny O'Kane's home in Dooish.

Firing for winter was won on the steep hillside above the road leading to the rocky path down towards the hollow where the house was nestled against the hill. I often saw Conall carefully pick his steps downwards from the mountain bog with a 'burden' creel on his back heaped full of hard black turf. Occasionally, of a winter's night the entire contents of a creel might be emptied on to the hearth creating a mighty blaze, the furnace heat of which left one's shins sizzling while the biting wind that whistled beneath the door cum half-door turned the calves of one's legs to ice.

A BURDEN OF TURF
(*Simon Coleman rha,*
for the irish
folklore commission)

Downdraughts could sometimes be so powerful as to fill old-style houses to such an extent that it would be impossible for a visitor to discern the identity of individuals sitting round the fire, their upper bodies being totally enveloped in smoke. That sort of thing could earn a community the nickname 'Smoky-heads', as was the case in regard to the good people of Westmeath, for example. No such problem existed in *Teach Eoghain Phádraig* as far as I know.

The outshot bed was also a feature with which I was familiar from home. Beds of this sort were situated as close as feasible to the fire, in a nook jutting out from the normal line of an outer sidewall – hence the description 'outshot' – and curtained around the side and end for privacy. Typically, older people and those who were sick, resorted to them for warmth and company and convenience. They could also be the deathbed of an ailing family member and the bed on which their corpse might be waked.

The only time I saw that particular outshot bed occupied

was one day when, to my surprise, I happened to find Pádraig Eoghain Phádraig lodged in it. Unusually, neither Máire nor Conall were to be seen anywhere. He responded to my enquiry as to his health by remarking in that forthright way of his, *'Tá an bás agam!'* – 'I am dying', then produced a half-full five-noggin bottle of whiskey from beneath the blanket and took a long swallow from it. He told me that once, many years before, he had felt so poorly that he was sure he was lying at death's door. I suspect Pádraig may just have had a very heavy cold but whatever his ailment that day, history repeated itself and neither it nor the whiskey brought about his demise on that occasion.

It could well have been that day that I raised an issue I had pondered now and then, which I felt Pádraig might prove to be more inclined to address while on his own. Could he speak English I asked. 'Yes, I could once', he declared (in Irish), 'but I have forgotten it!' – *'Bhí aon am, ach rinne mé dearmad air!'* He must have been one of very few Irish people to have learnt English and then let it all fade from his memory again in the course of the twentieth century!

Otherwise, the sleeping arrangements in that household remained a mystery to me. I would imagine there was a bed or two in the lower room, one of them perhaps a settle bed, and also some sort of 'shake-down' on the half-loft.

Seán Ó Eochaidh, who knew the family well, once told me the following story of a house visit paid by their local curate of the day who happened to be his nephew. The curate adjourned to the lower room to hear their confessions where he was first joined by Máire. She was duly shriven and after a short hiatus it came the turn of one of the two brothers, at which point the priest heard Pádraig pronounce as follows on the appropriate order of proceedings as he saw it: *'Gabh thusa síos chuige, a Chonaill agus coinnigh ag dul é go dtabharfaidh mise a chuid don ghamhain'* – 'You go down to him Conall and keep him going till I feed the calf!'

When the business of paying parish dues came to be settled Conall, once again at his older brother's behest, scuttled up the short ladder leading to the half-loft, and from a sack chock-full of money, withdrew a random bundle of old English five-pound notes which he thrust into the priest's hands. For all their apparent lack of worldly goods, they had no lack of cash.

The shift from pounds, shillings, and pence to decimal coinage – when 100 new pence replaced 240 'old' pence to the pound – brought havoc into their lives, exemplified by Máire's bafflement at what appeared to her to be a sudden drop in price of the groceries she purchased from Marley's travelling shop when it arrived on its weekly visit shortly after the new dispensation, of which they knew nothing, came into force. Máire was supposed to have been amazed at the reduction in price of her beloved tea and, believing this must have had to do with the nature of the product itself, is said to have commented: *'An bhfuil a fhios agat, tae beag an-mhaith atá inti!'* – 'Do you know she's a grand wee tea!'

During his time in *Na Cruacha* Seán Ó hEochaidh came across one of his valued informants hunkered bare-assed in the small garden beside his house, his fundament touching the ground here and there as he hopped from one location to another. This 'touch and go' technique was designed to test the temperature of the soil in preparation for planting potatoes, Seán was informed. Some parts of *Na Cruacha* lay in shadow even in the height of summer and the growing season could be short; striking a balance between getting the crop into the ground as early as possible, while running the rich of losing it altogether in cold and soggy ground, posed an annual dilemma. Many chose to circumvent the difficulty by participating in a process involving annual arrangements with Glenfinn farmers who swapped part of their ample crop of high-quality potatoes for sheep reared in *Na Cruacha* – an exercise in exchange and barter that worked to the benefit of both parties.

When I started my thesis research in the autumn of 1964, I took up residence in the heart of *Na Cruacha*, lodging in the friendly home of Bríd and Eoghan Muí in Cró Leac in the house in which the Donegal folklore collector, Seán Ó hEochaidh, stayed during his days collecting in *Na Cruacha* some twenty years before. Apart from brief stays in Fintown and Glenties, I spent about six months there, ranging from that base through the wild and beautiful country round about in my ancient Ford Prefect. Painstakingly, I went from townland to townland, logging all the data I could find about local placenames, big and small, and their associated lore. This field work provided the raw material for my thesis and for my first academic article, later published as 'Placenames of Inniskeel and Kilteevoge' in *Zeitschrift für celtische Philologie*, then under Heinrich's editorship.

In the hospitable Muí household, I joined in the winter pastime of playing cards, the favourite games being 'Twenty-Five' and 'Whist', in both of which I was well practised, having grown up in a household of inveterate card-players. The difference was, of course, the totally Irish-language ambience in which I had to learn not only the various technical terms, but also the art of participating in the abbreviated (and often subtly coded) commentary that formed part and parcel of these occasions. I became an Irish speaker like never before, my tongue even approximating to the drawl typical of speech in those parts.

As I made my way from place to place, often guided by one enthusiastic informant to the home of the next suitable interviewee, I would rattle off my introductory doorstep explanation describing who I was and what I wanted, not neglecting, of course, to mention the name of some helpful neighbour whose recommendation had led me there in the first place. My well-practised patter delivered in the local dialect produced many a puzzled look as people strove to place my face, convinced that I must be some class of local, yet looking for all the world like a total stranger.

On the western fringe of that Gaeltacht area, I once accosted a local who listened patiently to my patter and then politely observed in English: 'I understand every word you're saying but I can't answer you!' In another context, I once met a man of a similar disposition from the townland of Townawully, just over the hills from *Na Cruacha* on the south-facing escarpment of the Blue Stack Mountains. I sensed from his accent that he might know Irish so I popped the question directly to him: *'An bhfuil Gaeilg agat?'* – 'Do you have Irish?' His reply was just as direct as my question and even briefer: 'Naw, none,' said he!

Once, I met a man standing in the doorway of his house near Glenties. He listened intently to what I had to say in complete silence, looking me up and down with ill-concealed suspicion all the time. When I reached the end of my pitch, he addressed me as follows: *'Caidé an* constituency *go dtáinig tusa as?'* – 'What constituency did you come from?'

This abrupt interrogatory, complete with infixed English jaw-breaker, actually conveyed quite delicately his bewilderment as to who I was and his misgivings as to what my real purpose might be. It gave me to understand immediately that, before engaging with me, the poor man needed to be convinced that I was not a government spy, cunningly disguised as an Irish speaker, bent on denying him some entitlement or other. We speedily transcended that difficulty, but while he supplied all the information I needed for my ends, I never got past that particular doorstep, all the same.

On another occasion, I was taken for the A-I (Artificial Insemination) man, or *'An Tarbh Bán'* ('The White Bull') as he was called in Donegal, and directed towards the byre by an old woman who clearly could not tell the difference between a battered, black Ford Prefect and a white Volkswagen, from which the A-I man's Irish designation derived.

One local farmer became so enthusiastic about my work that he insisted on supplying not only the local names but full translations where possible, and highly dubious folk etymologies whenever the meaning of the basic Irish word elements was opaque and difficult to interpret. This fellow's observations extended to an utterly perverse analysis of the name 'Glenties', the anglicized form of *Na Gleanntaí* i.e. 'The Glens'. His reading of the name Glenties, however, insisted that the 'cover *mór gleanntaí'* ('the many glens') surrounding the town were all 'connect*áilte ag bun!'* ('connected or tied together at the bottom [of each glen]') – hence the name Glen-ties.

I was frequently obliged to revert to English as I approached the outer limits of the Irish-speaking districts. Here, while people still knew many of the placenames and could provide convincing renditions of them, a passive knowledge of Irish at best was the order of the day for most of the population.

On completion of my field work, I returned to Belfast to begin the task of writing up my thesis. My first port of call was Heinrich Wagner's office where I launched into a report of my long sojourn in Donegal. Heinrich listened intently without interruption to what I had to say as I talked and talked. At last I fell silent and, when Heinrich spoke, I realized that he had not been listening to what I was saying but rather to how I was saying it. '*Caithfidh mé a dhul ar ais go Dún na nGall!*' – 'I must go back to Donegal!' he blurted out, no doubt thinking back to his days in Teelin and Gortahork and the wonderful fluency in Irish he had acquired there.

The McAloons' other siblings had long since fled the nest, a sister to nearby *Cruach an Airgid* (Silver Hill) and a brother – '*Micí an Garda*' – left to become a policeman. I happened to be in the locality when another brother, Eoghan, and his wife returned from Philadelphia on a short visit. A reception party was organized and the entire community was invited to *Teach Eoghain Phádraig* in *Cruach Mhín an Fheannta*. The accordionist who lived next door, Patrick Rua 'ac a' Luain, and sibling members of Micí Mhicheáil Óig's family were there along with numerous other members of the wider McAloon clan.

In that crowded kitchen before a roaring fire on the open hearth, there was music and song and dancing galore, the latter featuring 'Maggie Pickie', a solo step dance performed by *Conall an Damhsa* 'Dancing Conall', Eoghan's younger brother.

CONALL *AN DAMHSA*

Later, perched on the short
stairs leading to the half loft,
Conall also played the fiddle
as did his kinsman Joe Beag 'ac
a' Luain, both protégés of the
famous Doherty brothers, John
and Mickey Simie.

CONALL PLAYING FIDDLE

I played my part by
ferrying Pat, Rodie (also
McAloon by birth), and Joe
Gibbons there and back in my
motor car to what was a kind
of 'convoy' in reverse, 'convoy'
being the term used to describe
what is elsewhere dubbed an
'American Wake', the farewell
prelude to final leave-taking and emigration. That evening was
also a 'last farewell', in a manner of speaking, for few of that
jolly crew were ever to convene again.

Joe, long a bachelor, eventually married Susan, a fine
woman from the parish of Ardara and they had two children.
Susan understood Irish perfectly, but rarely, if ever, spoke it,
while Rodie, her mother-in-law, was more than adequately
equipped in the opposite direction. The two women seemed
to enjoy a cordial relationship chit-chatting all the time
in different tongues, but it left visitors like me never quite
knowing which language to speak or respond in. Joe had at
last acquired a permanent English-language tutor.

Many years after that soirée, during a stay over Christmas
in Drumquin, my youngest brother, Declan, and I headed off
to *Na Cruacha* on a Christmas Eve visit. We found Pádraig,
Conall, and Máire by the fire and they made us welcome
and invited us to share in a few bottles of stout which they
had laid in for Christmas. We chatted, Conall played a few
tunes, as did Declan, who had brought his fiddle, and about
11 o'clock we said our farewells and made our way back to the
car parked a short distance away.

There we found to our dismay that the battery had been

totally depleted by a rear-window heater that had earlier been deployed against the night frost. The car in question had automatic transmission and, on that account, could not be started by pushing and so there we were stranded high and dry in the middle of the mountains. Declan and I began to step the road towards the next house some distance away, the towering peaks all round us etched against the starry sky.

Teach Eoghain Phádraig in winter

We were headed towards *Teach Eoghain Mhicheáil*, where Joe Beag 'ac a' Luain maintained a lonely existence as the last of the many inmates of that once-thriving family home, where only the younger members had learned English.

That house had been a favourite haunt of John Doherty (one of the famous Doherty brothers) who consented to record a few tunes for me one day I happened upon him there. One of these was an air *'Tá muiltín beag agam ar téad'*, of which I had only ever heard the words but not the music.

I hoped that Joe could be persuaded to drive us to the Reelan bridge where a telephone kiosk was located close to Josie Bonnar's pub. My plan was to ring Drumquin from there and summon assistance.

Joe did bring us to the Reelan bridge where we arrived minutes after midnight on Christmas morning. The pub was in darkness and we rightly surmised that all and sundry had left for Midnight Mass in Glenfinn chapel. Suspecting the same might be true of the family home in Drumquin, I hastened to place a call and, miraculously, got through almost immediately, just in time to nab the last straggler hurrying off to Midnight Mass in Langfield and deliver the SOS.

At last, we sighted the lights of returning cars advancing up Glenfinn, and when Josie appeared, I explained our dilemma to him. With little ceremony, we were ushered in and shunted into a little side room where a few embers lay dying on the hearth. A short time later, the ashes were cleared away, a fire put down afresh, and drinks were served.

Present also was a well-known fiddler of the locality called Jimmy Gallagher. Josie, who was mad about music, encouraged him to tune up and, knowing that I played the accordion after a fashion, asked if I would join in, declaring that he had a box upstairs which I could borrow. We maintained a vigil waiting for the rescue party to arrive from Tyrone and one tune followed another as Jimmy, Joe Beag, and I played.

The music was going strong, when, sometime in the wee small hours of the morning, my brother, Seán, appeared in the doorway. He had expected to find us without, sober and shivering, and was mightily astonished to find us seated within in high good humour, snug in front of a roaring fire, glasses filled to the brim. I nodded a greeting and as the last note sounded asked him if he knew the name of the tune. 'It could be "The Breakdown",' said he, with a smile. In due course, fully charged battery fitted, we turned our faces east and set a course for Tyrone as day broke over Glenfinn on Christmas morning.

My next meeting with Joe Beag happened long after that, at the funeral of Máire Rua Uí Mhaí, a noted singer of *Na Cruacha*, from whom much valuable material has been recorded. Following the burial, mourners adjourned for a meal to a hostelry in the nearby village of Brockagh where Joe Beag and a handful of other friends and I happened to share the same table. As the food was served, at first Joe seemed to hesitate. Then, he drew back from the table and seizing his plate placed it on his knees and began to eat. His solitary existence had led him to abandon formal dining practices and develop his own technique. The last of his kind in one of the few inhabited houses left in the valley they call *Na Cruacha*, I'd guess that gentle soul continued to dine off his knees until the day he was found dead, alone, in 2003.

Sadly, today, Irish-language songs are not much in vogue in Glenties, of which it has been said, as one man from *Na Cruacha* put it to me: '*Dá labharfá Gaeilg ar na Gleanntaí, shílfeá go raibh adharca ort!*' – 'If you were to speak Irish in Glenties, you would think you had sprouted horns!' Sadly, too, *Teach Eoghain Phádraig* is in ruins and the last of its one-time inhabitants in the clay.

Some of the recordings I made in *Na Cruacha* – of Pádraig McAloon in particular – have a more memorable history than others. Whereas Conall McAloon did possess a somewhat uncertain musical gift when it came to fiddling, he never sang a word of his father's songs, nor did Máire, as far as I know. But Pádraig made up for it all, for he was much given to 'singing' his repertoire utterly tunelessly, the rhythmical variation from item to item and, of course, the words, constituting the only discernible difference between one rendition and the next.

One winter's evening by that hearthside, Pádraig, in singing mode, delivered six verses in praise of a woman of outstanding comeliness whom he referred to as *Gráinne na gCuirnín* ('Curly-headed Grace'). The eponymous beauty was dubbed 'Gráinne Uí Dhuirnín' by Énrí Ó Muirgheasa, who had collected five verses of this love song near Dungloe in north-west Donegal, at least forty years before. Pádraig's title characterized this redoubtable female by her curls, but both his and Ó Muirgheasa's rendering

PÁDRAIG BEING RECORDED

of the words are at one in revealing this Gráinne to be not just a pretty face, but an accomplished lady of learning as well:

Canann sí Béarla agus léann sí Laidin,
Eabhrais is Gréigis is gach tréithre ban-ghaiscí.
Nach mór an díth céille domh a bheith ag dréim lena samhail
Is go dtug sí an chraobh léi ó Éirne go Leanainn.

(She speaks English and reads Latin,
  Hebrew and Greek, a featous female.
How foolish I am to aim for such as she
  Who holds the palm from Erne to Lennan.)

Late that night, I left them there and headed out of the mountains and down Glenfinn, making for my birthplace in Tyrone, just a few miles from the Donegal border. I was well pleased with my night's work and looking forward to reviewing the contents of my recordings the next day. Little did I know that I was to have the opportunity of doing so a lot sooner than expected.

I followed the road running alongside the River Finn, which I crossed at the junction separating the 'Twin Towns' of Ballybofey and Stranorlar, and then recrossed a little further on at Castlefinn before climbing up towards the border crossing at a place called Kilclean where stood the customs and 'frontier post' – as the British authorities curiously named their premises, like some outpost up the Khyber Pass.

All was deserted and in darkness. Wary of roadblocks and the possibility of nasty surprises (I was aware that cross-border gun-battles had taken place in the vicinity on a number of occasions), I eased my way across the narrow strip of no man's land. Suddenly, I spotted a number of shadowy figures emerging from the undergrowth on either side and a red light flashed briefly, signalling me to stop. My car was swiftly surrounded by soldiers, their blackened faces near to invisible in the pitch dark night.

I was asked the usual questions by a crisp English voice demanding to know where I was coming from and where I was going to, then ordered at gun-point to open the boot and bonnet while the interior of the car was inspected. I told them my journey had originated in a place called *Cruach Mhín an Fheannta*, a revelation that appeared to be of little interest to them for all its euphony. Certainly, it appeared not to be as interesting as my Uher Reporter 4000 – then one of the most sophisticated portable tape recorders on the market – neatly enclosed in its pigskin case and innocently perched on the back seat.

I was asked what was in the package and ordered to open it. I said it was a tape recorder and unbuttoned the flap to reveal that this was indeed the case. Perhaps, the officer imagined that he and his men had happened upon some cunningly disguised explosive device, or maybe he was just not au fait with the latest in sound recording equipment. One way or another, he remained unconvinced and without further ado I was instructed in no uncertain terms to make 'the package' play something – presumably, if his suspicions proved correct, running the risk of blowing up myself and all around me in the process.

I swiftly thumbed the rewind key and pressed 'Play'. There, in the Stygian darkness of that lonely hilltop, Pádraig Eoghain Phádraig began to howl his encomium for 'Curly-headed Grace'. The soldiers did not say what they thought of the recording, the song, or the singer sounding off in a language that the stranger did not know – to paraphrase a lesser, if better-known, ditty. However, Pádraig and I had done enough to convince them we were both harmless and I was allowed to pass on my way, my precious cargo intact. Today, that recording forms part of the National Folklore Collection and this little story of how it came to be there now also forms part of the record for posterity.

Infuriating hold-ups at British Army permanent checkpoints were the bane of our lives. Undoubtedly, these would have been explained by the authorities as a necessary precaution, but ordinary punters generally viewed them as being based on the principle of causing as much disruption as possible to people's lives by being deliberately dilatory in processing each vehicle, thus causing long tailbacks. It was harassment in any man's language.

The Aughnacloy crossing from Monaghan to Tyrone, which accommodated much through-traffic to County Donegal, was notorious in this respect. Travellers bound for Donegal were destined to suffer a second long wait at the Strabane-Lifford crossing further north. I think I am right in saying that one old man lost his life while a front-seat passenger stuck in the queue at Aughnacloy. He was quietly smoking his pipe when the sun caught the silvery band surrounding the bowl and a jumpy squaddy shot him dead.

Once my brother Declan and his companion musicians, inordinately delayed there, decided to while away the time by having an impromptu open-air session while they waited. Other motorists and their passengers were pleased by the regalement provided but, for all that, it was a foolhardy act for they ran the risk of being gunned down for their efforts. On another occasion, my brother, Seán, and I – like numerous other fans on the way to a match in Clones – were detained by a Fermanagh roadside for no apparent reason until the match was well and truly under way and then waved through.

By and large, however, the soldiers themselves were not particularly aggressive nor, indeed, it must be said, were they particularly thorough at some checkpoints. At one such on Boa Island, County Fermanagh, I took to presenting my driving licence as I drew to a halt and proffering it to the waiting squaddy before it was requested from me. The soldier would then take a gawk at it, hand it back to me and wave me on. Not having been afforded the opportunity

SÓC with British Army soldier, Belfast 1970

to formally ask me for my licence in the first instance and, since Irish driving licences at that time bore no photograph, the poor man had no way of knowing if the licence was mine. In addition, the printed text on the licence was mainly in Irish, as was my name and address which had been handwritten by some official or other in an almost illegible scrawl. On another occasion, a keen-eyed soldier while searching the boot of my car spotted my wife Maj's name on the label of a suitcase, shot to attention and saluted, saying, 'Major in the Irish Army, then?' One look at me should have told him immediately that I was no military man much less a Major in any man's army. In the Irish army, 'Majors' are called 'Commandants', but one could not reasonably expect a son of English soil stranded on a foreign shore to have been aware of that distinction either.

In the early years of the 'Troubles', a mobile army patrol intercepted me near the Aughnacloy border crossing and I was quizzed by another keen-eyed but more intelligent soldier, who scrutinized my licence closely, and then completely wrong-footed me by pointing to part of the hand-written, Irish-language address, asking, 'What does that word mean?' My address at that time was '9 Páirc na bhFeá' and, as his finger hovered over the word *'bhFeá'*, I stammered (assuming that the curious combination of upper and lower case letters it contained was what had caught his attention) – *'bhF'*, pronounced like a 'v' – never imagining that he could be intrigued by the meaning of the word *'Feá'* ('Beech') itself. 'I know, I know,' said he (hopping over my failure to answer his original question), 'I have the Gaelic.' It was then I registered the Highland Scottish accent and understood that, though a member of an English regiment, he was a Scottish Gaelic speaker.

Instantly, our roles were reversed and I was asking the questions from then on. He said he was from the Outer Hebridean island of North Uist, which I knew a little of, having visited there as a student, and we chatted back and forth for a while in Common Gaelic as best we could. As I sailed off down the road, I could see him pointing in my direction and chatting animatedly with his colleagues, no doubt recounting details of our encounter. I hope he survived his tour of duty among the 'Sea-divided Gaels' (to quote Myles na Gopaleen) of Ireland.

This experience contrasted sharply with an incident involving the Royal Ulster Constabulary (RUC) when I made another visit to the North in the early 1970s. My wife, Maj, and I, together with my father and mother and my brother, Seán, and his wife Ella, had motored from Drumquin to Omagh for a night out in St Enda's GAA Club. As we neared our destination, we were confronted by an RUC checkpoint. A female constable, paper and pencil in hand, asked to see my driving licence and earnestly set about transcribing the details. As these were well nigh impossible for her to decipher, I volunteered assistance and spelled my name for her letter by letter. She then started on my address and, at that point, I informed her that the address on my licence was no longer relevant as I had moved house and so another spelling session ensued. Having made a careful note of everything and the customary examination of my car boot having been carried out, we turned into St Enda's car park and made our way into the clubrooms.

Maj Ó Catháin & King Billy, 1970

Shortly after, a loudspeaker announcement called for the driver of car number so-and-so (my car) to go to the door. The doorman, who happened to know me, told me the police were waiting for me outside and that he would keep a weather eye on things. On exiting the club, I was surrounded by armed police and ordered to hand over my licence by a pugnacious senior officer who immediately accused me of having earlier refused to give my name when requested to do so. I insisted, of course, that I had given my name and that I had even spelt it to boot. His next challenge left me in no doubt as to what he really meant: 'You refused to give your name in the language of the country,' he barked. Clearly no linguist he or lover of Irish! I bit my tongue, gathered my wits and told him it was the only name I had, no matter the country.

I was then frogmarched to the nearby police Land Rover where, sitting within, I spotted the female constable who had earlier taken down my details so assiduously.

'What address did this man give you?' said the officer, clutching my licence all the while.

'Fourteen...,' she began, before being interrupted by her superior.

'It says "nine..." here,' he hooted triumphantly.

The constable graciously explained away the discrepancy, whereupon I was led to my car, the innards of which were then torn apart – side-panels, seats and flooring. They drew a blank, of course. Having hammered everything back into place, I was asked to sign a declaration that no damage had been caused. Needless to say – not fancying a night in the clink – I duly signed, and that was that. Welcome to Northern Ireland, how are you!

VII

A Queen's Postgraduate

I N 1966, the work was completed and my thesis submitted for examination. The extern examiner was Professor Myles Dillon, a Celtic scholar then attached to the Dublin Institute for Advanced Studies. White smoke emerged in due course and in 1970 my thesis was published in *Zeitschrift für celtische Philologie*, the prestigious Celtic journal of which Heinrich was then editor.

As the Ministry of Education had sponsored the research, and as the university had insisted that I be registered as a student under the name stipulated on my birth certificate, the authorship of the article was duly credited to James O'Kane. It is the only one of the hundred and more articles and books by me over the years to sport this designation. Not long after, I effected a name change by deed poll. So having been known in Irish-language circles for many years as Séamus/Séamas Ó Catháin, I became Séamas Ó Catháin for good, except for my *curriculum vitae* and the pages of the *Zeitschrift* where the recorded authorship of my first published academic article will always remain 'James O'Kane'.

Either name would have been valid currency south of the border, of course, but in the North these names were effectively deemed to be as different from one another as Cassius Clay and Mohammed Ali. Executing a deed poll was the only option open to me while resident in the North and I had no hesitation in taking the step that condemned me to a lifetime of spelling my surname letter by letter in the allegedly bilingual Irish State which ultimately became my domicile.

Fate took a hand in my final months as a postgraduate student at Queen's. I was contemplating what the future might hold for me when – out of the blue – the post of Research Assistant to Heinrich Wagner became vacant and he offered me the position. This brought not only enhanced status, but also the handsome salary of £800 per annum. It also entailed a modicum of teaching duties as laid down by Heinrich plus privileges as a member of staff with his foot on the lowest rung of the academic ladder. Field work with Heinrich in Donegal was one of the perks I enjoyed as he completed the very last entries for his *Atlas*.

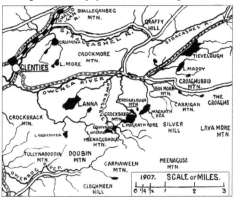

In this context, I piloted him to an isolated townland called Doobin, near Glenties, which I had visited during my peregrinations in those parts. It lay roughly between *Na Cruacha* and E.C. Quiggin's Meenawannia. We trekked across fields to an isolated, beautifully kept, old thatched house where we met with a warm welcome from a young couple and their children together with the young woman's aged mother. The old woman was a linguistic gem and the main target of Heinrich's interrogation based on the standard questionnaire used in his *Atlas*.

The problem was her difficulty in understanding English, particularly the foreign accented variety spoken by her inquisitor, and so her daughter, anxious to ease her mother's concerns, volunteered to mediate the process. Heinrich would pose the question – 'How do you say "X"?,' the young woman would immediately interpolate *'Cad é mar déarfá "X"?'* (or simply utter whatever word or phrase constituted the answer). Her mother would then deliver her response, mostly replicating her daughter's words and exact pronunciation.

Now and again, however, quite startling deviations would crop up due to generational dialect differences between the two women, as exemplified by the following exchanges: 'How would you say "the people of Ireland"?' – *'Cad é mar déarfá "bunadh na hÉireann"?,'* the young woman piped up and quick as a flash her mother added, *'Sea, bunadh na hÉireanna'*, instinctively substituting the older genitive case for the shorter one favoured by the daughter. Likewise, the answer to the question, 'How do you say "Wait till he comes"?' was batted across to the old woman as, *'Fan go dtiocfaidh sé'* and her linguistic reflexes spontaneously converted it to *'Fan go dtigidh sé'*, deploying the old subjunctive in preference to the future form. She maintained her dignity through all of this, mystified and all as she was by it, but Heinrich was delighted by her performance, of course. Such is the staple diet of philologists and what makes their hearts beat faster!

We were entertained to tea, bread, country butter, and a *gogaí* (boiled egg) apiece and then sat chatting round the fire while Heinrich puffed contentedly at his pipe until eventually it seized up. No pipe cleaners were to be had, but the young woman of the house resolved the issue by capturing one of her hens and – to much squawking – abstracting a conveniently-sized feather from the unfortunate bird. It was a memorable day in many ways.

Not long after Heinrich had landed in Ireland in the mid-1940s, he had been earmarked by the Dublin Institute for Advanced Studies (DIAS) top dogs as a likely candidate for taking on the mammoth task of conducting the field work for the *Linguistic Atlas and Survey of Irish Dialects* (or LASID). As part of his induction, he was despatched, in the company of Professor Myles Dillon of the DIAS, to Tourmakeady in the southern end of County Mayo where they were to make some initial probings, having first identified suitable informants adept in the local dialect.

Heinrich and Myles were not cut from the same cloth. Heinrich had been of the opinion that they might do the business in jig time over a few pints in the local pub. That was not Myles's style, however, and Heinrich described how they spent the day to-ing and fro-ing here and there, returning empty-handed, tired, and hungry to their hotel in Ballinrobe. As they entered, Myles turned to Heinrich and said, in that anglified way of his – 'I say, Wagner, how about a spot of veal?' The waitress was summoned and veal was duly ordered for dinner.

In the immediate post-war years, veal was not a common dish perhaps anywhere in Ireland, and the unfortunate waitress returned in due course to inform them that chicken was the one and only offering available. On hearing this, Myles turned to Heinrich

BALLINROBE, Co. MAYO

and – to the latter's astonishment – declared in disgust: 'Savages, Wagner, still savages!'

Heinrich's heroic endeavours in successfully executing the *Linguistic Atlas and Survey of Irish Dialects* were to earn him the opprobrium of the Irish-language movement, who bridled at his description of what he met with in the field as the 'ruins of a language'. It was a realistic assessment, for he had travelled the highways and byways of Ireland seeking out the last native speakers wherever he found them in order to systematically document the idiosyncrasies of the many all-but-extinct local dialects as well as other less threatened varieties of the language. More hurtful to him, perhaps, were the snide criticisms of some Irish scholars who were quicker to find fault than they had been in agreeing to participate in the gargantuan task essayed by the young Swiss.

Thenceforth, my life would be bound up with Heinrich Wagner's until his unfortunate demise at the relatively early age of 65. I was not only his Research Assistant, but also remained his student, attending various courses of lectures he gave from time to time. One such was a series of lectures – a real tour de force – on the typology of world languages, at which I took extensive notes, subsequently typed up while the information was fresh in my mind.

The branch of linguistics called structuralism was not to Heinrich's taste to say the very least. In a sense it was not so much that he was not convinced by the theorizing of Noam Chomsky et al but rather that he did not derive sufficient scholarly satisfaction from it. For him, I fancy, that kind of stuff amounted to little more than paddling about in the linguistic shallows when he always liked diving in at the deep end. This was a dangerous way of doing things, of course, and he could and did make the odd belly flop. When he was right – and he often was – he was brilliantly so and when he was wrong, he was never afraid to admit his mistakes.

Heinrich possessed a musical ear, probably the best natural talent that a phonetician could wish for. He had after all once set his heart on becoming a concert

HEINRICH WAGNER WITH ANNIE MCCREA
AT GREENCASTLE, CO. TYRONE

pianist, and only took a serious interest in academic pursuits upon recognizing that he simply would never be good enough to reach the pinnacle of his ambition in the music profession. But Heinrich was more than just a phonologist, for he also possessed an extraordinary ability to identify and penetrate the inherent genius of languages, both ancient and modern, discerning their inner structure and absorbing their lexicon at bewildering speed. His broad linguistic horizons made him a formidable philologist whose intellect and imagination set him head and shoulders above most of his Celtic Studies colleagues in Dublin, some of whom made little attempt to conceal their lack of admiration for his talents or achievements.

All in all, Heinrich was an inspiring figure whose presence in Belfast opened up vistas of other worlds beyond our ken.

Some of his students, myself included, followed his example by going abroad to try our academic fortune elsewhere and all who did so achieved success. For my part, I confided in Heinrich that I wanted to continue with Celtic Studies at a foreign venue, possibly at one of the great continental centres like Paris or Bonn. He told me that I was the first of his students to express such a wish and that he would be delighted to see what could be done by way of finding the finance for such a venture.

Official encouragement for engagement with Celtic Studies abroad from a local base was nonexistent and so Heinrich began the rounds south of the border. In many ways, his confession of failure was hardly surprising since Northerners like myself tended to be left out of the loop, so to speak, in terms of eligibility for suitable scholarships, which were in any case extremely limited in number and, as like as, not already spoken for. His abortive attempts to tap into funding of that sort led to him resorting to lateral thinking and taking a completely different tack. The idea he came up with was to change the course of my life in more ways than one.

Heinrich's appearance in my room in the Celtic Department would have fascinated anyone interested in kinesics. Unusually for him, he seemed ill at ease shifting from one foot to another, as if he were the bearer of unwelcome tidings. There was to be no scholarship, but all was not lost, he explained, for as his Research Assistant I could be despatched on an extended mission abroad, drawing down my salary as usual for the duration – that's if I was willing to accept the assignment. Lapland, said he, where he himself had once visited, would be the place; there it would be beneficial for me to add another string to my bow by immersing myself in a completely different language culture. It was an astonishing proposal by any stretch of the imagination, but one I did not have the slightest hesitation in accepting there and then.

Relinquishing my services (such as they were) was not a problem, nor was his trusting me to take off on a solo mission, disappearing over the horizon far beyond his line of vision.

His first priority was to introduce me to the Lappish language and its Fenno-Ugric cousins. Some years before, he had spent a month or so in Norwegian Lapland in a small town called Karasjok, smack in the middle of Finnmark, Norway's most northerly and easterly province, and he had sojourned in southern Finland for a spell seeking to come to terms with its language too. Two other Fenno-Ugric languages – Mordvin and Cheremiss — were not entirely beyond his ken for he had studied them with Ernst Lewy, a former Professor of Philology at the University of Berlin, exiled from Hitler's Germany and living in Dublin. In short, he knew what he was talking about.

Heinrich's approach to Lappish followed exactly the same pattern as with the (radically) different dialects of Irish he had mastered in double-quick time – nothing less than hand-to-hand engagement in the front-line trenches. In Karasjok, he told me, he joined some locals in saving the hay and in drinking in the local hotel. The latter ploy backfired somewhat, however, when one of his best buddies was barred from entry even under Heinrich's patronage. If I remember rightly, Heinrich seemed to suggest that, as a Lapp decked out in his colourful traditional costume, this individual was not welcome in such an august establishment as the Karasjok hotel of the day. This may well have been true of Finnmark in the early 1960s, while the harsh official programme of Norwegianization was still in full spate, but, in fairness, it could well have been for other reasons too.

We set to in the autumn of 1967 with weekly sessions in his home, where, armed with Erkki Itkonen's *Lappische Chrestomathie mit grammatikalischem Abriß und Wörterverzeichnis* and Eliel Lagercrantz's *Synopsis des Lappischen*, my education began afresh. Heinrich had chosen the Lagercrantz volume for several reasons, one being because it featured Lappish texts together with phonetic transcription and German translation. Another important consideration stemmed from his having identified the Varanger peninsula in East Finnmark as an area of special interest, lying as it did on the extreme north-eastern fringe of Northern Lappish, which was the most widely distributed of the many dialects of that language (spoken in Norway, Finland and Sweden). It also bordered on the Kola peninsula in modern-day Russia, then forming part of the Soviet Union, where various East Lappish dialects held sway. I also signed up for an informal course in Swedish for interested staff members given by Ron Finch, a lecturer in German at Queen's. It was the only Scandinavian language available there in any shape or form and I saw it as a way of breaking the Nordic ice, as it were, reckoning that whatever little knowledge I gained might prove useful in some way or other once I penetrated the Far North.

Once Heinrich's in-built sub-atomic language particle splitter swung into action, I was subject to a cascade of detail about the typical features and intrinsic nature of Lappish, including an overview of its grammar and syntax. This was not so much a lesson in how to speak the language, but more to help me get my head around at least some of its alien qualities such as a superabundance of case endings, medial mutation of consonants, vowel harmony and postpositions, to mention but a few of my problems. It was, on the other hand a consolation to learn that Lappish has no verb 'to have', but in common with a range of other languages, both related and unrelated, it uses the same periphrastic construction as Irish – '*Tá X agam*' – 'There is X at me' = 'I have X'.

Heinrich spared no effort in helping me to a modicum of understanding of how Lappish functioned, and I had reason to bless his name many a time and oft after that for all the trouble he went to on my behalf. We also perused a map of Scandinavia upon which he had marked the key concentrations of Lappish speakers in its northern reaches and the kind of dialects they spoke.

That was more or less as far as his directions extended as to how actually to get to these places. It would not be much of an exaggeration to say that Heinrich merely indicated that having got to Stockholm I should turn left and continue as far as Haparanda, a border town on the Gulf of Bothnia, then turn left again heading for Rovaniemi, the northernmost railhead in Finland, then left again by bus for points north.

Rather alarmingly, the roads marked on Heinrich's map seemed to peter out soon after Rovaniemi on the Arctic Circle, which left me wondering what might lie in store for me in seemingly uncharted territory.

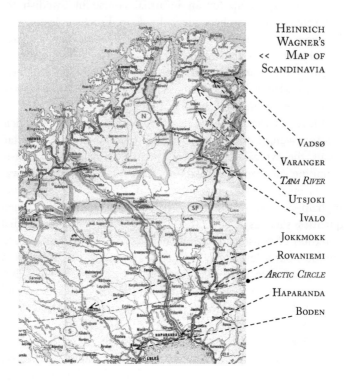

HEINRICH
WAGNER'S
<< MAP OF
SCANDINAVIA

VADSØ
VARANGER
TANA RIVER
UTSJOKI
IVALO
JOKKMOKK
ROVANIEMI
ARCTIC CIRCLE
HAPARANDA
BODEN

VIII

Beyond the Arctic Circle

M Y DEPARTURE had been set for early spring 1967, following correspondence between a man called Karl Nickul and myself. His name had been tendered by the Finnish Embassy in London as someone who might be willing to offer good advice, being the secretary of an organization called *Lapin Sivistysseura* 'Lappish Cultural Society' (of Finland). Karl had informed me that he would be in Stockholm at the beginning of March 1967 for a few days, departing soon thereafter for the annual conference of a Swedish organization called *Svenska Samernas Riksförbund* ('The Swedish National Lapp Association') to be held in Jokkmokk. I was welcome to rendezvous with him in the Swedish capital and join him for the overnight train journey to the north of Sweden where, he said, I would meet with Lapps not only from all over Sweden, but also from Finland and Norway.

The aboriginal population of Lapland is generally known to the outside world as Lapps, a denomination often perceived within Scandinavia as having negative connotations. Nowadays, they prefer to be called Sámis (from Sámi) and their domain to be called *Sámieatnam*, or Sápmi (= Lapland). This covers a vast swathe of country running from the Kola Peninsula in the far north-west of Russia, westwards along the Arctic coast of Norway and southwards and westwards through Finland, Sweden, and Norway, stretching far below the Arctic Circle. They are citizens of four different countries: today, there are about 40,000 Sámi in Norway, about 20,000 in Sweden, about 5,000 in Finland, and some 2,000 in Russia.

I could have had no better mentor than Karl, a native of Estonia, but a man who had spent most of his life in Finland, part of it sentenced to prison for his avowed pacifism during the war years. He was a geodesist by profession and, following the cessation of hostilities, he served on the body charged with drawing up Finland's new frontier with her erstwhile enemy, the Soviet Union. The Russians believed him to be sympathetic to their cause, but nothing could have been further from the truth, for he was a patriot, and a true friend of both the Finnish and Lappish people.

Between the wars, he had served in Petsamo, a narrow corridor that opened onto the Barents Sea giving Finland access to the Arctic Ocean, and had become closely involved with the Skolt Lapps of the Kola peninsula. He took a scholarly interest in many things including placenames, an area of common ground between us, and he was a prominent figure in Lappish affairs not only in Finland but elsewhere in the Nordic world. It was a happy circumstance that brought us together and one which was to have a decisive effect on the formation of my future plans.

Following the redrawing of the frontier after the war, Finland lost its maritime territories to the north, and elements of the Skolt population were relocated to Finnish Lapland, settling around the shores of Lake Sevettijärvi. About that time, Karl and his wife adopted a little Skolt girl who later married a member of one of Finland's best-known Lappish families, Oula Näkkäläjärvi. Oula was one of the many Sámi people I would meet with during my one and only visit to Jokkmokk.

Finland, in dire economic circumstances, sought to do its best for the Lappish refugees and Karl was much involved with the resettlement programme. They were grateful for all the help they received, he said, but complained bitterly about the quality of the water – probably among the purest in Finland – as opposed to what they had been used to previously.

My arrival in Stockholm on Saturday 4th March 1967 had marked my first visit abroad (apart from Scotland and the Isle of Man, if they count). My brief stopover at Heathrow airport before boarding my SAS flight for Stockholm had been my first time in England. My sister, Sheila, then nursing in Northampton, travelled to London to wish me *bon voyage*.

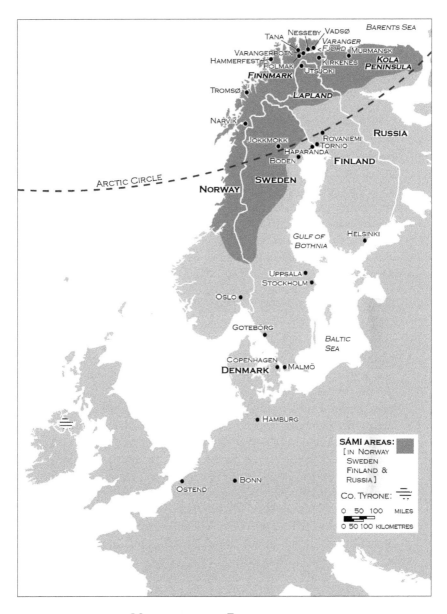

MAP OF NORTHERN EUROPE WITH THE
SÁMI REGIONS OF NORWAY, SWEDEN,
FINLAND, AND RUSSIA SHOWN SHADED

After parting, I adjourned to the toilet where I donned woollen underwear leggings, commonly referred to as 'long johns', in preparation for entering the big freeze. The heat they generated made my plane trip a highly uncomfortable experience and, on landing, I lost no time in divesting myself of them as soon as I could.

While I was in Karl's company in Stockholm, he was visited by a young Finnish Lapp from near Utsjoki, in far northern Finland, who worked in Gothenburg. Karl and he chatted together in Finnish. He was curious about me and, through Karl, asked me about various things including whether or not I thought it likely that I would run into some polar bears up north. My genuine response to the effect that I simply did not know, caused him to explode with laughter.

Later Karl helped me to book a seat and berth on *Nordpilen*, the night train from Stockholm travelling all the way to Narvik (on the Norwegian coast), by means of which we would make our way to Jokkmokk.

I had landed in Sweden armed with the names of two individuals with a Donegal connection, or at least a connection with my old friend, Seán Ó hEochaidh of *Gort a' Choirce*. One was a Swedish writer called Axel Liffner who, Seán told me, worked for some Swedish newspaper or other. Seán had met him during a prolonged stay in Donegal where they enjoyed each other's company in the comfort of McFadden's Hotel.

A few phone calls later I found him at *Aftonbladet*, one of the two Stockholm evening papers. He invited me to meet him there and we promptly adjourned to *Operakällaren*, a nearby upmarket drinking hole favoured by journalists. Afterwards he invited me to dinner with his wife and daughter at his house in the suburb of Bromma. Years later, Seán presented me with a small volume of Liffner's Swedish verses, containing poems written by him in Donegal.

Seán had got to know the second individual, an Anglo-Scot called Gordon Elliott, when Gordon and a friend, Birgitta Bucht, had managed to get themselves marooned by stormy weather on Tory Island, off the north Donegal coast. I managed to find Gordon in the Stockholm telephone book and arranged a meeting at his apartment where he introduced me to Birgitta, a native of Haparanda. Gordon made a living teaching English at various locations in Sweden and doing Swedish/English/Swedish translations. My acquaintance with him would last until his death in 2005. Birgitta enjoyed a highly successful career at the United Nations and, happily, is still to the good and in regular contact with my wife and myself. She invited me to stay at her father's house in Haparanda should I pass that way on my way north.

A couple of tasks remained, the first being to load up with liquor which, Heinrich had warned me, would be harder to get hold of the further north I travelled. Accordingly, I adjourned to the premises of *Systembolaget* (the Swedish state-run liquor monopoly) in Drottninggatan where I purchased, at considerable expense, two bottles of whiskey and a bottle of brandy. I buried them deep in my commodious rucksack which, in addition to my bits and pieces of clothes, also contained a bulky Grundig tape recorder. All in all it weighed a ton.

I was and always have been an Irish passport holder and my last job was to report to the Irish Embassy, which I had been advised to do before disappearing off the radar. The ambassador, Valentin Iremonger, a much-admired poet as well as diplomat, agreed to see me that evening at his residence in Engelbrektsgatan. I received a courteous welcome and gave an account of my purpose and my plans. I fancy he was somewhat at a loss as to what to make of me and I wonder if the few notes he took ever found their way into some government file or other. Thankfully, I never had any cause to bother him again.

I slept soundly in my bunk berth as *Nordpilen* ran smoothly through endless forests and snowy vistas reaching next morning the little station of Murjek where the bus to Jokkmokk awaited. Karl and I were booked into a modest bed and breakfast where we shared a room. He arranged for me to be enrolled with the conference and soon I found myself surrounded by variegated Sámi costumes and an equally diverse babble of dialects from all over *Sámieatnam* interspersed with Swedish, Norwegian, and to my surprise Finnish, which many of the Lapps seemed to use as a lingua franca.

The proceedings themselves might have been interesting to a degree had I been able to understand something of what was going on. Much of it, I gathered, had to do with reindeer husbandry, Swedish state regulations of one sort or another in that domain, and compensation issues in respect of animals which fell victim to passing rail traffic, or so I was told. Karl was a well-known and respected figure and through him I was introduced to all sorts of movers and shakers in the Lappish world, among them a famous Swedish Sámi called Israel Ruong whom I would later meet in Uppsala where he lectured at the university. I also met Karl's former son-in law, Oula Näkkäläjärvi from Inari (Finland), and most significantly from my point of view, Nils Jernsletten, a native of Tana (Norway), then studying for his doctorate at the University of Oslo and later to become the first Professor of Sámi language at Tromsø University.

Nils it was who supplied me with various names and addresses dotted along either shore of the Varanger fjord – the only one of Norway's many fjords opening to the east – including that of Siri Dikkanen, a native of Bergen who had married Olav Dikkanen (a Sámi man from Varanger). She spoke English and had recently published the fruits of her research for a Master's thesis on the social anthropology of salmon fishing rights and practices on the Tana River at Sirma. Siri sounded exactly the sort of person I needed to advise me.

The conference duly wound its way to a conclusion, the grand finale being a dinner sponsored by the Municipality of Jokkmokk. There were speeches and *yoiks* (the Sámi style of singing) and I was asked to sing an Irish song. Whether it was my singing voice or a sufficiency of drink – more likely the latter – I became the object of attention of a man who determined that I should abandon my plans to visit Varanger and learn Sámi in his home village of Övre Soppero (in northern Sweden) instead. It was a spontaneous and kindly gesture, and hugely welcoming in its intent. Nevertheless, I felt obliged to stick to my plan and rejected his offer to his obvious disappointment. Somehow, I felt that I was among friends.

The operation of the hotel bar dramatically underlined the rigorous Swedish liquor policy in keeping alcoholic beverages as far out of public reach as possible. I happened to be lurking nearby at the appointed hour when the door of a huge wall safe located behind the bar was ceremoniously unlocked by the manager and spirits of every description began to be painstakingly retrieved from the vault within and ranged along the shelves. Subsequently, the evidence of what had been on offer would be removed and the restoration of good order guaranteed when all temptation had been firmly placed behind lock and key once again. A comical business, indeed, or so it seemed to me, but I didn't see anybody laughing. I thought of Heinrich's friendly caution and the dear-bought stash I had hauled all the way from Stockholm and what might become of it.

In due course, Karl and I retraced our steps by bus to Murjek and thence by train to the important railhead of Boden where we boarded a modest railcar bound for Haparanda, the easternmost station in Sweden. We were headed due east, along the shores of the Gulf of Bothnia at the northern extremity of the Baltic Sea. We parted company at the railway station in Haparanda, half-twin of the Finnish town of Tornio on the far bank of the Tornio River. Karl's in-laws lived there and he would pay them a visit on his way back to Helsinki. We had enjoyed each other's company and I was sad to see him go. His enthusiastic engagement with me had opened doors and secured a footing for me in a world of which I had previously stood in almost total ignorance. I promised to write and let him know how things panned out.

The layout of the railway station in Haparanda introduced me to another intriguing reality of life in those parts. The station house and hotel – *Järnvägshotellet* – stood bang in the middle with different sets of tracks on either side. The line from Boden ended there just as the other line marked the beginning of the Finnish rail system running on the broader Russian gauge – all the way to Vladivostok, if one were so inclined and had the necessary permits to enter the Soviet Union. Here was one of the few points of contact between

Russia and Germany during the First World War, Finland at that stage being a Grand Duchy of Russia, on the cusp of achieving independence. A plaque in Tornio railway station commemorates the passing through it of no less a personage than V.I. Lenin en route to St Petersburg in April 1917. Through this same portal, Sweden – during the Second World War – provided respite for upwards of 80,000 Finnish children seeking refuge from the conflict engulfing Finland but, by the same token, facilitated German army rail traffic between occupied Norway and Finland.

I spent a day or two in the Railway Hotel and another few days in the family home of Birgitta, the Haparanda girl I met in Stockholm. She and her father and brother were very kind to me, showing me the sights and generally making me feel at home. Birgitta's father introduced me to the institution of the sauna, complete with birch twigs with which, in traditional style, one flagellated oneself – not by way of kinky punishment but in pleasant stimulation of well-sweated skin. One of the most curious sights I have ever witnessed was the roundabout border crossing between Haparanda and Tornio where the switch from left-hand traffic (Sweden) to right-hand traffic (Finland) produced a whirligig of weaving and dodging vehicles swerving across the frontier at breakneck speed in both directions.

It was two weeks and a bit after I left Ireland when I boarded the northbound Helsinki-Rovaniemi night train on the final section of its route from the Finnish capital to the main urban centre in the Finnish province of Lappi or Lapland, lying just on the Arctic Circle (66.5°N). There, outside a railway station whose main hall was strewn with inert bodies, weary travellers, homeless people, and drunks, I found a row of buses drawn up readied for departure. I stumbled along the line through the snow, map in hand, checking out the various destinations displayed, finally settling for one reading 'Utsjoki', one of the most northerly settlements in Finland. I climbed aboard not knowing how long the journey might take or where exactly it might end. The driver plucked a handful of Finnish currency from my extended fist and issued a ticket to

Utsjoki without comment. Some Norwegians used that service to take a short-cut to Oslo via Finland and Sweden. Like myself, most of them would not be conversant with Finnish.

That long passage, covering in excess of 400 kilometres, lasted from six in the evening until three o'clock the following morning, included various stops along the way in places like Sodankylä, Ivalo, and Inari as well as a number of roadside comfort stations. The bus had a radio – a novelty as far as I was concerned – tuned to a Finnish station. In the midst of a news bulletin, the voice of the British politician, George Browne, brought the highly unwelcome news from my budget's point of view that the pound had been devalued by 14%.

At one of the comfort stations, I opted to try my hand at Finnish, tuning in closely to a fellow passenger's order and observing that his request for 'maito' saw a glass of milk being delivered. The results of my efforts were mixed to say the least. 'maito' worked a charm, but when the woman behind the counter requested what turned out to be a reasonable supplementary clarification of my order I was completely flummoxed. 'Iso vai pieni?' she kept repeating, until eventually realising that she needed to hold up two differently sized glasses to illustrate the point. 'Milk, large or small?' my first four words of Finnish, taught me more than just vocabulary.

The bus thundered on through the night, shedding passengers here and there as it went, until eventually the driver and I were the last two aboard. The studded winter tyres made light of the snowy conditions, though I still drew comfort from the walls of snow ploughed up on either side of the road which I reckoned might provide a useful cushion in the event of a mishap. Lit by the headlamps, here and there at rises in the road I could see the empty landscape stretching far ahead. I decided to interrogate the driver and took up a position just behind him perched on the engine cover. We had no common language and hardly a common vocabulary of any sort, but he kept repeating 'hotelli' which I rightly assumed to mean that sooner or later I would be deposited somewhere I could find a bed for the night.

And so it came to pass that the bus pulled up outside *Utsjoen matkailu hotelli* – the Utsjoki Tourist Hotel – which lay in darkness. The driver stepped out and, affixing his thumb to the doorbell, held it there until the door was eventually opened by a sleepy-headed female who without further ado promptly led me to a vacant room. My journey was over for the day and I fell exhausted into bed.

Next morning, the manager gave me details of the Finnish bus service which he said would rendezvous with a Norwegian bus at the border. 'On the border' would have been a more accurate description for both buses were drawn up alongside one another on the frozen surface of the River Tana. Postbags and passengers were exchanged wordlessly and I sat in the Norwegian bus pondering its possible destination. I produced my map – the one marked up by Heinrich Wagner – as the driver approached and pointed to one of the places he had underlined. The driver shook his head. I tried another and again the driver shook his head. Only one possibility remained and this time he nodded enthusiastically. *'Seisson og femti'* ('Sixteen fifty'), said he, as I rooted out a few Norwegian notes of rather unwieldy denomination from his point of view and a handful of loose change which I had obtained from the Norwegians I met in Jokkmokk. The driver carefully counted out the change which amounted to exactly sixteen crowns, just fifty øre short of the fare and then waived the balance and handed me the ticket. Welcome to Norway, I thought.

The road ran partly along the frozen surface of the Tana River and partly on the regular dirt road, now, of course, covered with compacted snow. The houses here and there on either side seemed buried to the eaves in snow, likewise the sparse settlements occasionally visible on the Finnish side of the river. In the evening light, I caught a glimpse of the narrow contours of the Varanger fjord, and then the first open water I had seen since leaving home – the effect of the Gulf Stream. It made an unexpected sight and a welcome relief from all the solid ice I had experienced everywhere from Stockholm northwards.

NESSEBY IN NORTH-EAST FINNMARK

The bus halted by the roadside and the driver announced that we had arrived in Nesseby. He helped me unload my rucksack and, somehow or other, I understood that he wanted to know where I intended to take it from there. 'Dikkanens' I blurted out. 'Over there' (or words to that effect), said he, pointing towards a house a short distance away. I hoisted my rucksack as I watched his tail-lights disappear in the gathering murk, then tramped across the road to a house that, as I approached, appeared to lie in darkness. Journey's end, I thought, but what on earth would I do for my next trick if there was no one home?

Sure enough, my knock went unanswered. I lowered my rucksack to the low platform by the door and plumped myself down beside it wondering what my next move might be. The first thing to do was to hold my nerve, I told myself, the next to hope that my luck would hold and so it did. Round the corner of the house as if from nowhere came a man with a great swish of skis and wearing a Sámi costume. He stared at me in wild surprise as I tried to explain my presence. In broken English, he assured me that I could unburden myself with greater ease to his wife who was following along behind and whose English was much better than his. A few minutes

later, she appeared also on skis, wearing a harness and towing
a couple or more small children in a small covered sleigh.
This was Olav and Siri Dikkanen, the couple whom Nils
Jernsletten had recommended to me in Jokkmokk. The date
was 22nd March 1967, Spy Wednesday of Holy Week, and I
had parachuted into their lives from nowhere.

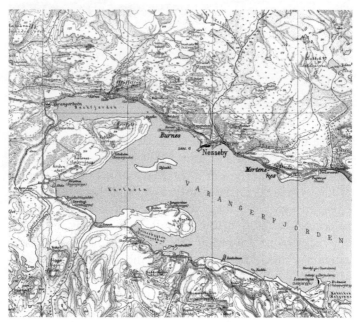

NESSEBY, BURNES, & VARANGER FJORD

IX

At Large in Lapland

THE FRIENDSHIP of Olav and Siri Dikkanen was spontaneous and the help they gave immediate, effective, and necessary. I stood ankle deep in snow, dressed about as inappropriately – from my low shoes to bare head – as I possibly could have been, and clearly in need of shelter and good advice. I got both in spades. A bed for the night, a bite to eat, and the reassurance that the task, which had been unexpectedly landed on them, of finding a suitable base from which I might commence my language studies would be taken in hand forthwith. Siri was a schoolteacher and, with Easter approaching, she and Olav had arranged to set off the next day to celebrate the holiday with some friends in Tana. They would leave by the morning bus. A speedy resolution was needed to this dilemma and once again fate intervened to provide an answer to the problem.

It happened that Erik Schytte Blix, the local Norwegian Lutheran pastor, was then serving out his last months in Nesseby before moving to Tromsø, and a meeting had been called for that evening to decide how his departure might best be marked by the community. Olav readied himself for the meeting dressed in his Sámi finery, Siri fussing around him, tweaking at his costume, making sure he looked his best. It would be a large gathering, she said, and Olav would liaise with people about me and my plans.

On his return, Olav was pleased to announce that not one, but two, local families had indicated their willingness to cooperate.

Next morning we boarded the bus together and a kilometre or so down the road I alighted and trudged up the hill to a small wooden bungalow looking out over the fjord. I knocked, but there was no reply. Then I ventured to open the door and entered a hallway leading to a cosy kitchen where a little woman sat by a small table. She was alone and, apparently, not expecting visitors. I was offered coffee and cake and given to understand that her husband was out but would be back soon. When he returned, it became obvious that the commitment he had given the previous evening had slipped his mind entirely and his poor wife had been left completely in the dark as to what was afoot. Such was my first meeting with Marianne and Karl Lindseth in their home at Burnes where I was destined to spend most of the following twelve months.

Karl (1891-1975) and Marianne (1903-1976) were in their sunset years, having reared a large family of two boys and six girls, the last of whom had flown the coop the year before. One of their two sons, Thomas (1929-2012), lived nearby with his wife Elen Bertha (1920-2002) and their family of five, four girls (Solbjørg, Torill, Ellen, and Astrid) and a boy, Thomas Kristian. They were later to become six in number with the birth of a second son, Per Gustav. Karl and Marianne's home was what was known at home in Tyrone as a '*céilí*-ing house' i.e. a point of informal assembly for neighbours and passers-by.

Karl was out and about a lot of the time, being the proprietor of a one-man local taxi service. This generated a lively traffic through the house. For all that, my unannounced arrival brought a promise of company for both of them, which was particularly

KARL & MARIANNE LINDSETH

pleasing to Marianne. We speedily reached an arrangement for payment of a monthly stipend for full-board and lodging. I was allocated a small but comfortable room just off the hallway and kitchen, and began to settle in. The house had running water, but no bathroom or lavatory; the outside toilet, in the good old-fashioned style, was fine except that it was wide open to the east wind at the rear, a circumstance that concentrated the mind wonderfully and dictated short sits when the wind blew from that direction. I had the run of the house and was treated as one of the family. Visitors came and went, some puzzled by my presence and wondering what I might be up to, others silently sizing me up from a distance. For my part, I had no words and my own silence must have compounded the air of mystery. The fact that my pencil and notebook were always at the ready to scribble down anything I could make out must also have added to the speculation. One of the first days there, Elen Bertha stepped forward to greet me and seizing my hand, on one finger of which I wore a signet ring, posed the following question – '*Leat go náitalam?*' I deserve no prizes for guessing from the context that she wanted to know if I was married, but, perhaps, some credit (thanks to Heinrich) for recognizing the past participle of the verb 'to marry' – '*náitalit*'. A small triumph.

People hurled words and expressions at me as I struggled to note them down phonetically. They would then ask me to read back aloud what I had written, as often as not breaking into hysterical laughter because of its obscene character. They were very outspoken and not the least embarrassed about anything, so I let them have their fun and kept writing, repeating, and learning. Burnes was Sámi-speaking, like the rest of Nesseby, but most people also knew at least some Norwegian and there were some non-Sámi families, most of whom tended to be monolingually Norwegian-speaking. A few, like Karl, also knew some Finnish, the language of the so-called Kvaen minority (or *Laddelaččat* as the Sámi called them) dotted at various locations around the fjord. But Sámi predominated in every household in the immediate vicinity and I did not doubt I had chosen the right place to become acquainted with *Sámegiella*, the language of the Sámi people.

In those days, the state operated a policy of Norwegianization with regard to the Sámi people, and Norwegian was the only language tolerated by officialdom. This meant that the young Lindseths – who like pretty well all the youngsters in that place spoke Sámi at home – were compelled to undergo their primary school education through the medium of Norwegian, following the same syllabus and using the same textbooks as their coevals in Oslo. Siri Dikkanen asked me on a number of occasions to visit the local school and speak English

SÁMI WOMEN & CHILDREN, NESSEBY, 1950S

with the pupils. I always took the opportunity to point out to them that, when it came to pronouncing English correctly, they had a significant advantage as Sámi speakers over monoglot Norwegians because they were already familiar with certain key sounds such as *th-* (as in *this*) and *th-* as in *thing*), not to mention the *ch-* and *ju-dge* sounds in *church* and *judge*, which cause Norwegian speakers endless trouble. Effectively, the schoolteachers – most of them from more southerly and westerly parts of Norway – were the only people in the place who did not understand the Sámi language.

Norwegian government policy gradually changed for the better and education through the medium of their own language became a reality for Sámi children. Today, there is a lively Sámi publishing industry providing textbooks and otherwise servicing local government and court services. While still in harness at University College Dublin, I had the pleasure of welcoming to Dublin members of 'The Sámi Non-Fiction Writers and Translators Union' who opted to hold their Annual General Meeting there. They were astonished to see the highly valuable collection of books about Lapland, the Sámi people, their language, and folklore that forms part of the folklore library in the National Folklore Collection at UCD.

Shortly after settling in, I had my own brush with Norwegian officialdom when a man arrived on skis one evening, appearing out of the dark with a lamp attached to his forehead. His name was Nils Banne and he had come all the way from the local police headquarters where he held the rank of Deputy Sheriff (*Lensmansassistent*). Somewhat unusually, he was a Sámi himself, and appeared to be an agreeable fellow – at least he and Karl seemed to get on well together. He was interested to know all about me and I showed him my passport and did my best to explain what I was about,

A few months later, Karl arrived back from one of his jaunts bearing a message from the Sheriff himself that there was some form or other that needed to be filled in and would I call in to him at my convenience. I was anxious to dispose of the business right away, but Karl dismissed this notion and there the matter rested. Another month or so passed and the Sheriff's form arrived. The form – an application for permission to remain in Norway – was duly filled in and despatched to local headquarters. I had travelled through Sweden and Finland on a three-month tourist visa, which had now expired and I needed to get right with God or hightail it back to Ireland. In due course, my passport was returned bearing no sign of an official stamp of any sort and no permit attached. I can only assume that the issue was resolved at local level and no further action was deemed necessary.

That part of the world being the highly sensitive sort of place it was during the Cold War, with the Soviet Union and Warsaw Pact armies ranged against NATO's best along Varanger's eastern extremity, and the ever-present threat of enemy submarines and of enemy agents in people's minds, it was no wonder an innocent abroad like me should have become the subject of attention. This had not been in Heinrich's script, of course. I learned *inter alia* that, not long before my arrival, a spy ring centred on a fishing port not far away had been uncovered and a number of Norwegians convicted of spying for the Soviets. And, of course, had I not arrived there myself on no less a day than Spy Wednesday itself!

I was left in peace and nothing ever came of this, though two curious things happened that may or may not be connected with my lack of official status. I had purchased a decent camera in Ireland and took numerous photos of people and places in my immediate locality, including of emerging spring flowers and the like, and endless views across the fjord to the snow-topped hills south of which lay the Republic of Finland. At regular intervals, these were sent off to Kodak in Oslo in the usual way for processing. Then came a hiatus affecting two rolls of slides, one of which, according to Kodak, never reached them and the other, according to Kodak, had been despatched by them but never reached me. I never saw either again.

In addition there were photographs I had taken on the island of Vardø in the mouth of the Varanger fjord overlooking the Murman coast. Karl and Marianne's youngest daughter, Aud, lived with her husband and several small children. It was a place festooned with antennae and aerials and all sorts of military installations and out of bounds to foreigners, a fact of which I was completely unaware. Karl and Marianne liked to visit their youngest from time to time and I would accompany them as an honorary member of the family. In those days, a ferry carried travellers across the short stretch of water separating Vardø from the mainland – nowadays, there is a tunnel. At any rate, I would pass the time by wandering unhindered about the harbour and all around the small town taking photographs of whatever caught my fancy. I wondered sometimes if some of my various pictures may have ended up in the hands of the Norwegian Secret Service.

One of those fine sunny days, I was returning from the post office when I met a local woman on the road – a friend of the Lindseth family – to whom I had previously been introduced. She was in full costume, the strong colours of red and blue and yellow standing out against the sky, the open waters of the fjord, and the snowy hills beyond. She was Norwegian by blood and had married in to a highly respected local Sámi family. I struggled to answer as she said hello, my grasp of Norwegian insufficient to cope. Her salutation was simple enough, but the poor creature went through hellish contortions trying to explain herself to me until I finally got the point. It turned out all she said in salutation was *'Deilig vær'* – 'Lovely weather'. How she must have regretted her civility in electing to say hello!

While I made no effort to learn Norwegian, believing I must focus entirely on Sámi if I was to succeed in my mission, I began to pick up bits and pieces from eavesdropping on conversations, listening to the radio, and perusing *Finnmarken*, the local newspaper published in the town of Vadsø. Struggling through Konrad Nielsen's *Lappisk Grammatik* (which I had on loan from Pastor Schytte Blix) in Dano-Norwegian also served to broaden my linguistic horizons. By some sort of osmosis, I learned enough to do business in town, including my monthly visits to Vadsø Sparebank where a portion of my salary from Queen's was sent.

VADSØ

Some of the bank staff played a trick on me by forcing me to conduct my business with them in broken Norwegian, denying any knowledge of English. A Sámi friend told me years later that the bank staff in question were particularly amused by my pronunciation which was heavily impregnated with Sámi phonological features, such as systematic replacement of initial *b–*, *d–*, *g–* by *p–*, *t–*, *k–* sounds. Thus, for example, '*bra*' ('good') came out as '*pra*', and '*grus vei*' ('dirt road') came out as '*krus vei*'. One would be forgiven for thinking that bank staff should have had better things to do than snigger behindbacks at customers and, by extension, at their Sámi neighbours.

As my knowledge of Sámi improved, I set about making paper slips containing new words and expressions. I had purchased a number of school jotters and cut up the pages to make these slips, and soon I realised I needed a supply of rubber bands to hold them together. In due course, I found myself in the local store owned by a genial Norwegian called Ivar Dahl and run by him and his daughters. It was the kind of country shop once common in Ireland, selling not only groceries and hardware but various items of footwear and clothing as well. An inner bar and snug in the corner were the only missing features.

The shop was full of customers, mainly women, all taking an eyeful of the stranger in their midst as I waited my turn. My problem was that nobody had been able to tell me what the Norwegian for 'rubber band' might be and my small pocket dictionary was also silent on the subject, apart from citing *'gummi'* as meaning 'rubber'. This is also a slang expression for 'condom', though I was not to know that. When I placed my order, the outburst of hilarity that seized customers and staff alike was a sight to behold, compounded, no doubt, by the catalogue of energetic pulling and stretching motions I performed in the futile hope of clarifying the issue and rescuing the situation.

Desperately, I looked around the shelves and suddenly, in a chilled food cabinet, I spied packets of bacon bound together with stout rubber bands. It was no easy task to have the shop assistants adjust to my mysterious change of tack, as it must have appeared to them, but eventually I persuaded one of them to hand me some packets of bacon from which I removed a rubber band, holding it aloft in triumph for all to see. I felt I deserved a round of applause, at least, for having persevered in getting my message across and giving everyone a good laugh in the process, but I left empty-handed, for as it turned out no rubber bands were to be found nearer than Vadsø some fifty kilometres distant.

I became a regular visitor in various homes of the locality, especially that of the Lindseth family, Thomas and Elen Bertha and their children, which was a few hundred metres away. Unfettered

TORILL LINDSETH & FAMILY

as they are by convention, children are invaluable assets in language learning. They laugh uproariously at one's mistakes and rectify matters without embarrassment and their speech is natural and uninhibited. I learned a lot from my more or less daily interaction with the Lindseth youngsters. I was welcomed in every house without exception, even in those dominated by the strong evangelical ethos of Laestadianism, a kind of extreme Protestant sect. The home of Wilfred Noste and his brother Nils and his wife Anna was one such household. All three spoke excellent Sámi, the only problem being that they tended not to say all that much. But their hospitality said it all. In some extreme cases, Laestadians eschewed all sorts of frivolous worldly practices and pastimes, even curtains and such fripperies.

Another calling place was the home of 'Old Dudda' (*'Dudd-áddjá'*), or Tude Mathisen, a bachelor who possessed a gift for healing. He held the honorary title of *miráhkal doavttír* (or *mirakeldoktor*) – 'miracle doctor', and his services were much sought after. People travelled long distances from all over northern Norway to seek him out. I loved to sit in his little kitchen and listen to the conversations, some Sámi, some Finnish, some Norwegian, as his patients awaited the summons to Dudda's inner room. He told me in detail how he had acquired his talent for healing by more or less serving his time to a famous female healer who lived elsewhere in Varanger. In some respects this was quite an ordeal as, at

regular intervals during the process,
he had to submit to being stripped
naked and totally immersed in a
barrel of ice until the blocks of ice
eventually melted around his body.
He cured me once, but that is a
story for another day.

As my knowledge of Sámi
improved, I was able to successfully
eavesdrop on many a side-of-the-
mouth enquiry by callers to Karl and
Marianne's home curious to learn
something about me. *'Gii bat dát
olmmoš lea?'* – 'Who's that fellow?'

Mirakeldoktor Dudda

they would ask, to which Marianne, bless her, would proudly
reply as often as not *'Dat lea mu biebmogánda!'* – 'That's
my foster son!' Karl, on the other hand, especially when in
his cups, was wont to maintain, by way of answer to such
questions, that I was his son, begotten in Germany during
the War, who had sought and found his father. Either way, I
realized I was regarded as one of the family.

As if to copper-fasten my status, they and others would
assure me from time to time *'It don galgga ballat!'* meaning 'Be
not afraid!' In truth I was never afraid among those kind and
decent people though that remark might well have caused me
some anxiety if I had interpreted it as suggesting that something
nasty awaited me just around the corner that they knew about
but I didn't. Many years later, in not dissimilar circumstances,
the same comfort formula would be tendered me by equally
concerned and good-natured people in Erris, County Mayo,
the thrust of whose comment did not differ a whole lot from
that of the Sámi – *'Ní baol duit anseo'* – 'You're in no jeopardy
here!' they would say, affirming my station as a stranger safe
among friends. One gets a feeling that there is something
in these words that answers to the age-old business of
community responses in dealing sympathetically with outsiders.

A curious incident occurred in Utsjoki that reflected
another aspect of my situation. Waiting for a bus outside

the same hotel that had received me during the night some months before, I fell into conversation with a Sámi man in splendid traditional dress of the Tana variety. We chatted back and forth about the weather and such like and then he said – *'Leat go don donbeale olmmoš?'* – 'Are you a far-side man?' This question, inspired by my Varanger twang, was simply a polite way of asking 'Are you a Norwegian (Sámi)?' i.e. someone from over the border on the other side of the river. To him the Sámi were a people separated by geography and dialect features rather than international frontiers.

Finnmark, like the rest of Norway, had been occupied by Germany during the war and the remains of their army camp in Nesseby were still visible. A roadside monument a few kilometres short of Kirkenes on the southern side of the Varanger fjord marks the most westerly point of penetration by Soviet troops following the rout of the German forces at the end of the war. I often heard it said that a Russian had parachuted on to the tundra-lands of the Varanger peninsula (probably on a spying mission) where he remained until the war ended.

In common with other parts of Northern Norway and Finnish Lapland, huge swathes of territory were devastated as a result of the policy pursued by the retreating Germans, which involved widespread burning of dwelling houses and other property. A Norwegian film about this called *Brent Jord* (*Scorched Earth*) featured local extras including my friend the Deputy Sheriff, Nils Banne.

Finland's participation in the War was calamitous for it. First, the Finns had fought on the side of the Germans and then, following the signing of a disastrous peace treaty with the Soviets, were compelled, though poorly equipped, to clear the Germans out of northern Finland. They managed to accomplish this after much travail and stupendous loss of Finnish lives.

The northern front between the Soviet Union on the one side, and Norway and Finland on the other, remained fairly static for the duration of the conflict, but Finland lost Petsamo and her vital corridor to the northern ocean. Some Sámi were in the Finnish army and were noted sharpshooters. Others, it is said, spent the war, like their Sámi brothers on the Soviet side, shooting aimlessly in the air instead of shooting at each other – the kind of circumstance, one would imagine, that would have contributed handsomely to maintenance of the status quo.

On the other hand, my Varanger friends spoke with horror of the activities of special Finnish ski troops (probably including local Sámi) who would venture far behind the lines, descending on isolated Soviet communities and slaughtering everyone they came across. If these foolhardy individuals survived the trip to make the journey home, they would haul with them sacks containing the hearts of their victims as evidence of their success. One can imagine these bloody trophies scattered for inspection on the snow in scenes reminiscent of certain passages in ancient Irish sagas. This was corroborated by a knowledgeable Finnish friend whose only comment was to the effect that it wasn't hearts they fetched home with them but livers which were lighter and easier to carry.

The troops stationed in Nesseby and district were Austrians and did not behave at all badly according to what I heard. Local stories told of how the locals attempted to deceive them in different ways with varying degrees of success. One such described how packets of what purported to be margarine would be bartered for other goods, the packets being in reality pieces of wood cut exactly to size and wrapped appropriately. Another recounted the fate of a local man who, having sold the Austrians what he maintained was reindeer meat, was invited into the mess to partake of a feast of boiled dog specially prepared for him and which he was forced to eat at gunpoint. During the short months of summer, I occasionally spotted all-male groups of German-speaking tourists, whom I fancied to be army veterans revisiting the scenes of their youthful exploits and experiences.

Undergoing occupation by a foreign army is an arduous business at best that visits all kinds of difficulties on those who suffer it and brings all kinds of consequences in its train. As in other parts of Norway people were reluctant to speak of their experiences in those troubled years and one is left with the impression that people kept their heads down and that some, perhaps, may have conducted themselves with something less than distinction. For all that, I recall only one direct reference to a Burnes neighbour who was alleged to have informed on people guilty of listening to foreign radio news broadcasts.

I watched the onset of spring with melting snows and splintered ice floes sailing down the fjord towards the open sea. I witnessed the emergence of earth burned brown by early winter frosts and wet and sticky underfoot conditions that preceded the emergence of new grass and fields of flowers. I had been puzzled by the seemingly haphazard patterns of paling posts, the tops of which were to be seen zig-zagging here and there in the landscape. The disappearance of the snow revealed a system of connecting wires between them on which the hay would be strung to dry come harvest time. Once when wandering in the hills behind Burnes, I followed a tinkling cowbell-like sound until I came on a small stream where I found the last pieces of ice jostling round some rocks before making their escape downstream.

The break up of the ice on the broad expanse of the River Tana was another matter altogether. In Karl and Marianne's company I had become a regular visitor to the villages of Alleknjarg and nearby Polmak where three of their daughters lived with their husbands and families, all local Sámi people. They seldom travelled empty-handed but when possible brought supplies of fish fresh from the waters of the Varanger fjord. I was made as welcome as the fish there and greatly enjoyed my visits to Nils Eriksen and his wife Regine, Georg Eriksen (Nils's brother) and his wife Ingrid, both in Alleknjarg,

KARL LINDSETH

and Harald Erke and his wife Birgit in Polmak. Only the latter couple survive intact, Georg, his brother Nils, and his spouse Regine, having passed away.

The shallow waters of the Tana were frozen solid all winter and the river functioned as a main highway for vehicular traffic practically all the way to the sea. The spring melt reduced the river to slow-moving, massive, crashing, tumbling chunks of ice and spilled its shallow waters onto the surrounding lands on either side. It would be the month of June before the last vestiges of flooding disappeared and the river would be studded with fish traps specially designed to capture the salmon for which the river was famous. The boats used to navigate the river were flat-bottomed and of shallow draught. They generally used outboard motors but were also propelled by long poles according to river conditions.

In early summer, at Nils Eriksen's invitation, I made a trip upriver in one of these boats, branching off from the main river to follow the Polmak River running close to the Finnish border. We disembarked at a tiny strand and made our way to a small clearing where stood a one-room cabin, timber-built, but clad with sods. We were duly invited to join its sole occupant, a man who shared my companion's first name. Nils explained who I was and I listened as the two men exchanged news in their rich Tana dialect. When it became clear to our host that I was able to follow their exchanges, he turned to me and asked *'Gos bat don leat eret?'* – 'Where are you from?' I was flustered by this enquiry and wondered what meaningful response I might offer as I did not think the poor fellow would have any idea where Ireland was. For all that, I eventually answered *'Irlánddas'* – 'From Ireland'. Sure enough, the follow-up question revealed the inadequacy of his knowledge of geography when he asked – *'Lea go dat doppe Ruotas?'* – 'Is that somewhere in Sweden?' Clearly while a Sámi speaker, my accent was still foreign enough to warrant such a guess. At least he was headed in the right direction.

I met other characters during my visits to Alleknjarg including a local distiller who remained highly suspicious of me despite repeated assurance by Nils and Regine that I posed no threat to him or his trade. I was later to sample his wares to disastrous effect but that is another story. I spent one hilarious evening together with Nils in another local house where copious amounts of drink were consumed and *yoiks* delivered by our host who gave me a present of a beautiful Sámi belt he had made. Our host was continually berated by Nils for liberally sprinkling his Sámi with Norwegian loanwords, for which Nils maintained I had no use as I needed to learn the proper Sámi vocabulary.

One summer Sunday, I accompanied Nils to a Pentecostal service organized by local members of that church. They sang lustily in Sámi to guitar accompaniment and also preached in that language. The whole business wound up with church members questioning individuals in the small congregation as they moved among them – 'Dovddat go Jesusa?' – 'Do you acknowledge Jesus?' Positive responses were few and far between as far as I could judge.

Another evening was spent in the convivial company of the local postmaster and his wife in their comfortable Alleknjarg home. Both were local Sámis, he from Norway and she from Finland, a few kilometres to the south. She was proud of her status as a Finnish citizen and, in that context, for some reason or other, she happened to mention the name of Carl Mannerheim, the famous Finnish military leader and sixth President of the Republic (1944–1946). She was astonished that no one present except me had ever heard of him. She had been taught about him in school, she said.

Apart from Tana, I also managed to see quite a lot of Varanger thanks to Karl and his calling as a taximan which often saw me accompany him when ferrying patients to appointments at the hospital in Kirkenes. It was dirt roads all the way with only short stretches of tarmacadam surfaces making a brief appearance in the immediate vicinity of larger settlements. Karl would sometimes take a detour off the main drag to visit Bugøynes where there were many Finnish speakers (Kvaen) and he liked to call into a particular shop there to practice his Finnish with the owner. ⟋

The village of Neiden was another interesting place along

the way with its river and rushing waterfalls and tiny Orthodox chapel maintained by a small community of Skolt Sámi, most of whose brethern belonged to Kola on the other side of the Soviet border. The town of Kirkenes itself is located only a few kilometres from the border and, while occupied by the Germans, was heavily bombed by the Soviets during the war.

A *yoik* that I first heard in Jokkmokk on my way north commemorates in song many of *Sámieatnam*'s best known municipalities and settlements, Nesseby, Polmak, Utsjoki, Karasjok, Kautokeino and other places, each of these placenames being tagged with an appropriate epithet – usually highlighting some negative characteristic or foible of the local population. Thus, the people of Nesseby – or *Unjárgielda* – are characterized as *'Rimbi, Rambi'* – 'Limping, Limping'. In this context, the population of Sør-Varanger ('South Varanger'), or *Mátta Várjjat*, were designated *'Giella moivvit'* – 'Language mixers', arising from the fact that no less than five different languages were once spoken there – sometimes simultaneously it would seem! – Varanger Sámi, Skolt Sámi, Norwegian, Finnish, and Russian. Today, Sámi (of both varieties) and Finnish are in retreat, and Norwegian is taking up the slack, but Russian too, with the easing of visa regulations, is gaining ground. The street names in Kirkenes are now bilingually Norwegian and Russian and 'language mixing' of the old kind seems to be on the way out.

The nights grew shorter and shorter and the days lengthened until by midsummer there was no night at all and daylight prevailed around the clock. It was bewildering at first for the simple reason that people seemed to be constantly afoot, some about their business at all hours and others withdrawing occasionally from the fray to snatch a few hours sleep at unpredictable intervals. The landscape took on a mantle of green as lush and verdant as one might see anywhere, even in Ireland, and sheep and cattle, released from their winter confinement, grazed the hills and grassy knolls along the seashore. The leaves of the dwarf birch – the only trees to flourish this far above the tree line – were in full bloom and the last vestiges of snow vanished from the north-facing escarpment of the mountains across the fjord guarding the horizon to the south.

Hay-making season followed soon after and the crazy-paving pattern of wire and paling posts was soon hung with bundles of grass strung out to dry. Not long after, the berry-picking season began

SÁMI HOUSES & HAY-FENCE

and the hills and moorlands were full of people searching out the prized cloudberry plants with their golden harvest of vitamin C. The summer season was short, however, and by August the days had already become noticeably shorter and the first night frosts set in.

As well as jotting notes about this and that, I had begun to make sound recordings of local people and also commenced transcribing these as best I could. The Varanger dialect did not feature prominently in published matter and, belonging to the most easterly fringe of Northern Sámi-speaking territory, differed sufficiently from the more commonly featured main dialects of Northern Sámi as to force me in the direction of finding my own way of writing it down other than resorting to phonetic script.

I worked hard at this until eventually I managed to produce something that might pass muster. To seek an expert opinion, I sent a few of these transcriptions off to Asbjørn Nesheim, Professor of Sámi Language at the University of Oslo, whose name I knew from various sources. I mentioned in passing that my sponsor, Heinrich Wagner, had suggested that I might make a collection of terms connected with fishing and the sea, and that I had already begun to note down customs, beliefs and stories about mermaids and the like. Professor Nesheim's speedy response, indicating that he felt I was on the right track and making a decent fist of faithfully rendering Nesseby Sámi into an acceptable written form, gave me great heart. His suggestion that we might meet in Oslo to discuss matters also pleased me, and led to my decision to take a break from my work in Nesseby and head south again.

So, towards the end of August, I found myself once again outside the Utsjoki hotel waiting for the bus that would carry me south to the railhead in Rovaniemi from where I would reverse my steps to Haparanda and Boden and board the night train for Stockholm and on again by train to Oslo. The dwarf birch had already begun to register the shift in the seasons and the countryside had assumed an amazing orange marmalade coloured cloak as the sap retreated downwards to their roots and their leaves glowed golden in the autumn sun. The Sámi call this *ruški áigi* and the Finns *ruskaika*, both meaning roughly 'the russet time'. I saw something similar, but on a grander scale, in parts of east coast USA where it is called 'the foliage'.

Marianne, conscious as ever of my welfare, insisted on sending a supply of newly picked and freshly preserved cloudberries with me for sustenance on the journey and I whiled away the tedious hours of waiting to make my connections by spooning their contents into me at intervals. I felt I should have been an object of curiosity, but nobody appeared to pay the slightest attention to me.

Travelling in Finland was still a bit hit-and-miss as I struggled to unravel the mysteries of Finnish bus and train timetabling. Basically, this was down to the system of postpositions (as opposed to prepositions) favoured by that language (and also by Sámi). Words equivalent to 'to' and 'from' affixed to the end of nouns effectively functioned as illative and ablative case endings and sometimes this caused internal mutation that could utterly transform the appearance of the original word or name. For a novice like me, anxious not to board the wrong bus – literally not sure at times whether it was coming or going – this caused not a little anxiety and taught me much about Finnish grammar.

When I reached Oslo, Professor Nesheim greeted me enthusiastically, even extending an invitation to join him and his wife and daughter for dinner at their nearby apartment that evening, and helping me to purchase some relevant publications including Eliel Lagercrantz's *Sprachlehre des Nordlappischen nach den seelappischen Mundarten*. I later went through this, heavily annotating words and phrases it contained with the help of my Sámi friends.

A few years later, following his retirement, I visited Nesheim at his apartment. Although then beset by Parkinson's disease, he was as warm as ever and thanked me for coming to see him.

On my return journey, I stayed a few weeks in Stockholm with Gordon Elliott, whom I had met when I first arrived in Sweden. Gordon, a kind-hearted, larger-than-life figure (who sadly ended his days in poverty) was great fun and not a little irresponsible in many ways. Once, for example, he inveigled me into accompanying him to a lecture engagement where he was to give a talk about Ireland as a tourist destination. As an additional attraction, my role was to say a few words about the Irish language and the delights of Irish traditional music and song. We had a few drinks before setting out, and a few more on the way, and then Gordon informed me that the lecture was being held under the auspices of *Nykterhetsnämden* – the Teetotallers Association. Though not severely inebriated or even visibly under the influence, nevertheless we smelled of alcohol and, needless to say, our presentations met with a cool enough reception. I rather doubt if anything either Gordon or I had to say resulted in any significant influx of Swedish tourists to Ireland.

—X—

A Long Night

In mid-September I followed once more the now-familiar route northwards by train and bus, through Sweden and Finland, back to Finnmark. My onward bus journey from Rovaniemi involved an interesting encounter with some young Finnish women who crowded into the back seat alongside me. They had been celebrating something or other and were not entirely sober. Emboldened by drink, they set about interrogating me as to who I was and what I was doing in their country – or at least that was what I imagined them to be asking about, as I could understand but little of what they were saying nor, indeed, could they understand me.

As evidence of my alienage, I produced my Irish passport which at that time had slots for two photographs, one of which was occupied by my mugshot, the other vacant. This caused a deal of speculation and the Finnish word *vaimo* meaning 'wife' began to be bandied about. I fully understood the context and, somehow, understood that they were on the right track. I recognized the word from Sámi but at first found this rather odd as *váibmu* means 'heart' in that language. When I managed to get this across to them, the ladies found it very romantic altogether. Another language lesson!

Sister languages and even kissing-cousin languages often share items of vocabulary with similar forms (and even pronunciations) but different meanings, sometimes subtle and beguiling as in this case. To take a couple of examples nearer to home, Irish *uisce* meaning 'water' occurs in Scottish Gaelic where, however, it means 'rain', and *bean* means both 'woman' and 'wife' in Irish, but Scottish Gaelic prefers a totally different word for 'woman'.

Playing the percentages in this kind of game got me into

difficulty once when attempting to buy butter in Finland and resorting to the Sámi word in the hope that it might deliver the desired result. Confusion reigned, however, because of the semantic shift between my Sámi *vuodja* meaning 'butter' and the existence of a Finnish counterpart *voide* not meaning 'butter' but 'ointment' or 'grease'. *Voi*, the Finnish for 'butter' is obviously related but my *vuodja* was not close enough to clinch the deal, hence the standoff. Fortunately, I had the presence of mind to adopt a swift change of tack by asking instead for *láibi* which I knew resembled the Finnish *leipä*. Once the bread was produced I resorted to miming the action of spreading butter and duly effected a successful purchase. *Pace* etymologizing and fancy linguistic acrobatics, necessity proved to be the mother of invention on this as on many another occasion.

On my way back to Nesseby, Birgit Nilsen, a care worker from the old people's home in Nyborg whom I knew, boarded the bus and immediately engaged me in conversation. She had been extremely helpful in facilitating access to some of the old folks under her care from whom I had recorded local folklore and I also had made recordings of her aged father in their home. He had lots to say about *stálut* and *Čudit*, *gufihttarat*, and *eahpárač* and other otherworldly figures well known in Sámi folk tradition. Following my short absence, my responses to her were clearly somewhat lacking in fluency and she suddenly brought me down to earth by declaring '*Vuoi, vuoi go don leat čurbun sámegielain*' – 'My, my, how stilted your Sámi has become!' She was perfectly right, of course. It was time to buckle down to work again!

My second coming to Burnes was considerably less traumatic for Marianne Lindseth than my sudden materialization the previous March, and I was joyfully welcomed back almost as if my departure for Oslo had been a disappearance for good. I settled into my old routine, but suffered an immediate setback when I discovered that my Grundig tape recorder had been rendered *hors de combat* by leaking batteries that had devastated its innards. Fortunately, a lad from the neighbourhood had just returned from sailing the world as a merchant seaman and when Odd Lamm became aware of the dilemma, he produced a spanking new Tandberg tape recorder he had purchased from him and offered it to me on extended loan. The Tandberg was a good quality desk model, heavy and unwieldy compared to the Grundig, but welcome, nevertheless, in the circumstances. Odd's kindly gesture enabled me to continue recording from late autumn until the following March when I packed my bags for home. At least, they would weigh a little less as a result of my loss.

The days shortened more and more as the sun hung lower and lower in the southern sky which became a kaleidoscope of colour due to the extraordinary angle of its rays as it sank further below the horizon. As it tracked southwards, the orb of the sun would eventually fail to rise above the horizon, but the sky would remain gloriously illuminated for weeks to come by sunlight bending round the the edge of the world. For all that, the sun would not be seen again until well beyond the far side of Christmas, but winter darkness was never a total blackout.

Before winter set in in earnest, I decided to commission a pair of reindeer-skin boots from Margit Mathiesen, who lived a short distance away further up the hill behind Lindseth's. I dropped in now and then to watch her at her work and she described in detail how she went about selecting the various pieces and sewing them together with dried reindeer leg sinews. Round the ankle opening were the Varanger colours of red, yellow, and blue, and similarly coloured tassels also dangled from the tie cord sealing the opening.

These boots were warm as toast, but viable only in temperatures below -5°C or so as snow would melt on the soles and one's feet would grow damp. They had no heel and I had to learn to shuffle along or, like primitive man, walk on the balls of my feet. The flat sole consisted of two separate pieces of fur, the rough pile of each running in opposite directions, a cunning stratagem that made for good purchase on the surface of the snow. I also learned the knack of inserting tufts of dried sedge grass under my feet while donning the boots and also remembering to remove them for drying by the fire for use again the following day. One had to husband the supply of this specially harvested grass which had a sweet perfume and felt good underfoot. The bits of sedge grass I thrust up into the pointy curved toes of these boots are still to the good in them to the present day. Later I had a tunic in the Varanger style made for me by another neighbour.

SÓC IN VARANGER STYLE

The first snows lent brightness, as did starry skies and moonlight. The emerald green of the Northern Lights brilliantly darting here and there brought a dash of colour to the overall gloom. It was possible to sit by the window and identify people going about their business, sometimes distinguishing a vehicle by its familiar shape or sound or recognising individuals by their characteristic way of walking. I cannot say that I enjoyed the dark period, but neither did I find it upsetting. It was all completely new to me and I took each day as it came.

Once I came upon the young Lindseths playing in the snow and, apparently, shouting at the Northern Lights that were flitting across the sky above their heads by fits and starts. The capricious nature of this display engendered periodic shrieks from the children who would run headlong for safety as soon as there was any shift in the heavens, whereupon their mother, standing in the doorway, would order the children to desist from teasing the Northern Lights, warning that if they did not do so, the Lights would descend upon them while they slept and steal away their entrails.

The children were, in fact, taunting the Northern Lights using an age-old formula in order to rouse them to action and put on a performance for their benefit. The magic formula they used runs as follows:

> Guovssahas, guovssahas, *lippati, lippati*
> Buoide bihttá njálmmis
> Veahčir gállus.
> [Aurora, aurora, *lippati, lippati*
>   A piece of fat in your mouth
>   A hammer in your forehead.]

'Lippati' I have heard explained as referring to the sound of reindeer running on snow, but the significance of the other seemingly anthropomorphic gibes remains a mystery to me.

The problem of transporting the Tandberg tape recorder was solved by pressing what they called a *'spark'* or 'kick-sled' into service. This was just a chair on runners which one could boot forward on ice or compacted snow like a scooter. I would fix the machine on the seat of the chair and set off to visit here and there in the hope of being able to make recordings. The home of Aage Lamm, my friend Odd's uncle, was a favourite destination. More often than not I would also find Aage's friend and neighbour, Aamot Eikjok, there before me.

Aamot was a good talker and storyteller – indeed he was more than that for he had been associated with the Laestadian movement for many years as an interpreter at meetings where the preachers were Finnish-speaking. The Norwegian Lutheran Church operated a similar system where the sermon given by the minister off the altar in Norwegian would be translated simultaneously by a Sámi man in full regalia standing alongside him. By his own confession, however, Aamot's Finnish was far from perfect and sometimes, he said, when faced with some insurmountable difficulty, he would simply hop over the passage in question *'dego Holmenkollen'* – 'like Holmenkollen' (a famous ski jump near Oslo), as he put it. Another local translator /preacher was remembered for his rendition from the Norwegian of a phrase meaning 'I was born under the Law' as *'Mun lean riegádan luovvi vuolde'* – 'I was born under the *luovvi*' (an elevated wooden stand for storing hay and other produce), in which he transmogrified the Norwegian word *'lov'* (meaning 'law') to Sámi *'luovvi'*.

A SÁMI *'LUOVVI'*

Preaching could be a thirsty business and he and others spoke of a notorious alcoholic minister of the Finnish Lutheran Church in Utsjoki who, it was alleged, always kept a bucket of beer alongside him in the pulpit, bobbing up and down occasionally during the sermon to partake of draughts from its contents. Perhaps, this assertion may have been coloured to some extent by the differences perceived between high-church Finnish Lutheranism and the rather more low-church profile of Norway's state religion, not to mention general free-church tradition, including Laestadianism.

Be that as it may, the Varanger Sámi were highly suspicious of their fellow Sámis to the east – the Skolts or *Nuortalaččat* 'The Easterners' – whom they considered to be magicians and sorcerers. Perhaps, in part, this may have had to do with their adherence to the Orthodox Church, and maybe even also to their partiality to tea (in the Russian style) as opposed to coffee. Perhaps, the gulf between their two dialects of Sámi – almost wide enough to be thought of as two different languages – may have had something to do with it as well. In any case, the Skolts were seen as being different, even dangerous to a degree.

The following account by Aamot Eikjok illustrates the point. Some time between the wars, he and a companion set off on what the Norwegians call a *påsketur*, an Easter skiing trip, tracking far to the east along the southern arm of the Varanger fjord until they reached a place called Boris Gleb on the banks of the Pasvik River, then the frontier between Finland and Norway. They called into one of the houses in the Skolt settlement there and were offered hospitality in the form of tea which they gratefully accepted.

There they sat in their reindeer-skin boots and furs and drank cup after cup from the samovar until Aamot decided he had had enough and, having emptied his cup, promptly turned it upside down on the table by way of polite indication that he had had his fill. His companion, less well versed in local manners, however, neglected to follow suit and, when offered a refill, declined without further ado, thus incurring the wrath of the old Skolt head of household at such rude behaviour.

Suddenly, an invisible fly started dive-bombing the unfortunate ingrate's head, buzzing all around his face, but proving impossible to see or swat. The house was extremely warm and the visitors were sweating profusely in their furs to such an extent that a tiny mouse, thitherto happily ensconced in the collar of the fly-beleaguered individual, was forced from its hiding place and, behind his head, began a lively trot back and forward from one shoulder to the other.

Aamot's companion remained blissfully unaware of this unexpected display which was taking place in full view of the old head man. Almost immediately, the invisible fly disappeared, and shortly after the two visitors (and the 'magic' mouse) took leave of their hosts. Aamot interpreted this summoning forth of a fly as a demonstration of the old Skolt's magic power and, equally, his recall of the insect on the conjuring up of a superior rival apparition as recognition of his having been trumped by a greater magician than himself. Clearly, size mattered!

They skied for home up the steep snow-clad escarpment above the village, but as he reached the top, Aamot realized his companion had gone missing. He retraced his steps and discovered his friend lodged upside down, skis in the air, in a deep drift, from which he hauled him to safety. It transpired that the belt securing his mate's trousers had snapped and his trousers had fallen round his ankles, tripping him up and hurling him headlong into the snow. Trousers reinstated, they ascended to the cliff edge, whereupon the man who had taken a tumble turned and, looking down at the village below, pointed at the house they had just left and said – 'It was you old Skolt (*Nuortalaš ádjjá*) that did that to me!' They experienced no further interference after that, for once identified as the source of magical interference, the old Skolt was powerless to work any further magic against them.

I smoked a pipe in those days and my mother would send me occasional supplies of my favourite plug tobacco – Player's Digger if I remember rightly – and once, for some reason or other, a roll of vile and unsmokeable twist tobacco. It could be chewed too and I discovered a devotee of the art in my friend, Aamot, who tackled it with relish. I used to dole it out to him in small doses at our meetings in Aage's house, often drawing the comment from him that, if he kept this up, he might fall under its spell to such an extent that he would have to follow me back to wherever the dickens I came from when I finally left those parts. As a true Laestadian – which he can hardly have been – he should not have been indulging in tobacco products of any kind whether to chew or otherwise. He was a helpful, humorous soul who did his best to assist me in my quest for language and lore.

I kept up a regular correspondence with my mother and one or two other people and looked forward to her letters with news of home. One letter I received cast me into immediate despondency for it informed me that my father's mother – Granny O'Kane – had been buried two weeks before. As was the custom, she had been waked at her home, and so large had been the throng, my mother wrote, that they were forced to serve tea 'out on the street' i.e. the space around the outside of the dwelling house. I fancy that observation was by way of confirming that she had been a popular woman and her death had not passed unnoticed. I have no doubt that it was meant as a consolation, but in truth it felt like an accusation, as I was practically the only one who wasn't there to join in the obsequies and was left to mourn alone. A day or two later, I must have been caught staring at the floor and someone, rightly divining that I seemed a bit depressed, roused me from my contemplation of the space beneath my feet by jauntily inquiring *'Áiggot go eatnama oastit?'* – 'Are you thinking of buying land?' I was thinking of land alright, but far away. Much later I was told that my father had heard three mysterious knocks at the door the night of her death, a traditional omen of impending death among the Gallagher clan to which she belonged. She was a kindly soul who appeared to carry lightly the tragic loss of three of her children to the 'Spanish Flu' early in her married life, in 1918.

Aage Lamm was a soft-spoken, mild-mannered man, less flamboyant than Aamot but every bit as well-disposed towards me. My occasional jaunts to the local post office saw me pass his house along the way and as often as not I would call in to say hello. One such day, I found myself standing in his doorway when he suddenly became agitated and sternly advised me either to come in all the way or to stand outside, but not on peril of my life to remain in that in-between space, a place beset by otherworld forces, he said.

As Christmas drew near, thoughts of home weighed heavily on me and I longed to be with my own kith and kin from whom I had never before been separated at that holiday. I was determined, however, to see the year out and then try to complete as close as possible a full year in Lapland. Christmas shopping provided a distraction of sorts, especially the excursion Karl, Marianne, and I made to the modest emporium located in Nuorgam, metres inside the Finnish border where everything was so much cheaper than in Norway. My finances were limited, but in the end I decided to purchase a large case of American apples, ostensibly my only gift to all and sundry.

The nearest liquor store in Norway was located in Hammerfest several hundred kilometres to the east and, at that time, the nearest in Finland was in Rovaniemi, four hundred kilometres to the south. Beer could be bought more or less locally from a special store in Skipagurra some forty or so kilometres away. Shortly before Christmas, twelve bottles of assorted spirits arrived at Lindseth's house all the way from Hammerfest via the coastal steamer (*hurtig rute*), calling at Vadsø. This was a consolidated purchase put together by various households in order to avoid the cost of freight which was waived for orders of twelve or more bottles at a time. I had a trick up my sleeve, however, and did not subscribe to this particular plan of action as I had yet to broach my stash of whiskey and brandy bought in Stockholm the previous March. When all three bottles were handed over by me, their revelation came as a pleasant surprise to all concerned – an unexpected Christmas bonus. They were flabbergasted that I had managed to secrete such a cache unscathed for so long but were not found wanting in helping me to polish it off in record time. The load on my homeward journey would be all the lighter for it.

Marianne was quite abstemious, but Karl was partial to an occasional off-duty drink. He would sometimes fetch a crate of the excellent beer manufactured in Tromsø by Mack Øl from the special store in Skipagurra and I would sometimes rise to ordering some as well. Once while we were having a bottle or two at the kitchen table, I reached over to pour him a top-up. For convenience sake, I happened to do this by flexing my wrist over the back of my hand in order to empty the bottle into his glass. He immediately seized my arm and halted the process, warning me that I was pouring away the luck by decanting the beer in such a cack-handed way. On another occasion, we shared a beer or two at the kitchen table and when I felt I had had enough, I said goodnight and adjourned to my chamber. Some time later I was roused from my slumbers by Karl who maintained that we were far from finished yet and demanded that I rejoin him to complete the exercise. I wanted no more, but I sat with him until he self-administered the sought-after *coup de grâce* at which point I was able to beat a safe retreat.

Otherwise, as far as I know, he was not what people sometimes call 'superstitious', or much interested in anything other than cars and his taxi business. This, along with his courtship of Marianne (in which his car played a major role), was celebrated in a *yoik* extolling his exploits as Nesseby's *'boaresemus sjåføra'* – 'oldest chauffeur'. His mother, according to Elen Bertha and others, was another kettle of fish altogether. She was described to me as a woman, small of stature and stooped, of whom everyone went in fear because of her active belief in accompanying spirits – her *'noaidegázzi'* – that followed her everywhere. Sometimes, it was said, she could be seen waving her arms behind her batting away her spirits and ordering them to keep out of her way. She would also be seen brushing her skirts and tugging the hems, all the while admonishing her spirits to cease bothering her and then sweeping them out into the porch and ordering them to remain there. Thomas Lindseth told me that, as a child, when his grandmother climbed up to see him where he lay in the loft, he could hear her instructing her spirits not to follow her up saying that that was no place for them to be.

As elsewhere in mainland Europe and Scandinavia, Christmas Eve rather than Christmas Day is the main focus of seasonal celebrations, and Karl, Marianne, and I travelled to Tana to join with the family members attending the Christmas service at the tiny Lutheran church in Polmak. The church was awash with colour, most of the congregation, which was packed to the doors, being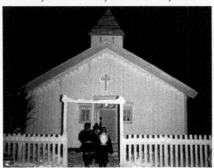

POLMAK, CHRISTMAS 1967

decked out in their splendid Sámi costumes, the women especially resplendent in their tunics, silken scarves, gold and silver brooches and pretty bright-red bonnets. By contrast, the minister presented a drab figure in his black and white robes topped off by an Elizabethan ruff around his neck. Standing alongside him, and outshining him by far in terms of his appearance, was the official interpreter resplendent in his finest Sámi outfit.

The sermon was a double act, the minister's remarks being broken into readily digestible sound-bites which were immediately translated into Sámi with practised panache by the interpreter. It was a very smooth performance by both men. The possibility of some lack of concordance between the two sermons, however, clearly existed, if the oft-repeated critique to the effect that the interpreter's efforts were generally vastly superior to those of the minister were to be believed

The coming of 1968 was remarkable for the gradual return of refracted sunlight over the horizon and then, in the last week of January, the reappearance of the orb of the sun and direct sunlight to light our dark world once more. Everyone should make a wish on first seeing it, I was told. The year 1968 also brought the advent of television or, I should say, Norwegian television, to Finnmark. For those who owned Finnish-bought television sets, Soviet television, broadcasting from Murmansk, was already an addition to people's lives albeit of dubious merit, consisting as it did mainly of war films. Truth to tell, Norwegian television programmes were not a great deal better, but they were at least more intelligible as far as I was concerned.

I remember an incident in the Lindseth living room one evening when one of the so-called 'hallo-girls', i.e. continuity announcers, appeared on our screens to describe some upcoming delight for the viewers. Suddenly, one of the young bucks present vaulted from his position seated on the floor in front of the television set and triumphantly planted a kiss on the screen, crying as he did so, 'See how I kissed the Norwegian dame,' or words to that effect. The Sámi word for 'kiss' – *cummá* (pronounced 'tsum-ma') – being wonderfully onomatopoeic and with a double -*mm*- that seemed to go on forever – lent something extra to his claim.

On another occasion, this same living room also housed a Pentecostalist service conducted by the group I had seen in Alleknjarg. With their permission I hung a microphone from the lampshade in the ceiling and recorded the entire proceedings. Neither Karl nor Marianne was particularly religious-minded, but had in all probability simply responded courteously to a request to allow a visit to their home for this purpose.

In similar vein, I listened one day to a lively debate as to who would take up the challenge of ringing the veterinary surgeon in Kirkenes in connection with an ailing sheep desperately in need of medical treatment. The burning issue was whose Norwegian was good enough to adequately describe what was wrong with the poor animal. The discussion ebbed to and fro until eventually Karl's son, Thomas, found himself elected to take on the task. To a rapt audience, he ran the techno-medical gauntlet with ease and, on hanging up, celebrated his success with whoops of triumph, jumping up and down, hands high in the air.

Sometimes, things did not turn out as well, as illustrated by one story of a local woman who had reason to consult a doctor in Vadsø and had been advised to carry with her a urine sample for analysis. She duly filled a phial of some sort as required and, somewhat abashed, on presenting it in the clinic, was heard to politely enquire in her best Norwegian – *'Ska denne podeln hjem?'* – 'Should I take this bottle home with me?'

What humour may rest in this otherwise run of the mill account arises from the unfortunate woman's invention of a new word for 'bottle' and her quaint conclusion regarding its ultimate destination. Without being too po-faced about matters, her instinct was to Norwegianize – in what she judged to be an acceptable form (*'podel'*) – the Sámi word *boahtal* (also meaning 'bottle'). Ironically, this perfectly good Sámi word is itself a borrowing from Norwegian *'butelje'*, in turn ultimately a borrowing from French *'bouteille'*: in other words, the sequence runs as follows – *podel = boahtal = butelje = bouteille.*

News broadcasts on the BBC World Service which I was able to hear intermittently on the Lindseth's radio kept me abreast to some extent of events in the outside world, while local radio in Norwegian and a daily short news and magazine programme in Sámi gave me occasional insights into local matters. Except for the news, people did not take a huge interest in the Sámi programmes emanating from Tromsø, which generally had little to say about Varanger and even less about Nesseby. Cultural coverage featuring *yoiks*, especially those from Kautokeino, sometimes drew howls of derision because of their lack of melody by comparison with *yoiks* in the Varanger style. These alien sounds made a poor impression, some people even going so far as to compare them to the yapping and yowling of barking dogs. I listened to all of it, however, and was also a regular listener to a weekly half-hour programme on Norwegian folk music broadcast from Oslo to which nobody but myself paid the slightest attention. I was always fond of music.

An unexpected bonus came with the advent of television, namely the screening of *Særlingen* – a Norwegian version of Brendan Behan's *The Quare Fella*. This play contains occasional passages of dialogue and songs in Irish all delivered in the dialect of County Donegal. I have no idea how this was engineered, but it was good to hear and set me thinking of my life and times in that far distant stamping ground of my youth. About the same time, Heinrich Wagner had written to say that he would be on sabbatical leave in Switzerland in the spring, and hoped to spend two or three days a week at the university in Bonn. He felt it would be a good idea for me to come to grips with German and suggested I make plans to join him there before returning to Queen's.

My upcoming separation from Nesseby was preceded by separation of another more spectacular variety, that is to say an annual assembly of reindeer for the purpose of sorting and selecting beasts for slaughter. Gathering the animals over a number of days was a slow and difficult process, but eventually they were all successfully corralled in a hillside enclosure between Varangerbotn and Skipagurra and the task of isolating reindeer from the circling herd, lassoing them, and dragging them aside for the cull began. *Boazo rátkin* (Sámi) /*poroerotus* (Finnish) /*reinskilling* (Norwegian) are the names applied to this practice.

The image of hardy groups of Sámi people eking out a precarious existence on the snowy wastes of northernmost Norway, camping under the stars here and there as they tend their flocks, is a throwback to a time before motorized transport and modern communications. Nowadays, long reindeer drives from winter quarters in the interior (such as the environs of Kautokeino) to summer pastures on the coast and islands of Finnmark are still a feature of the lives of some Sámi, but the vast majority lead a far less flamboyant existence.

The mountain plateau of Varanger accommodated thousands of reindeer that were tended by their herders and owners, most of whom lived in or near the shores of the Varanger fjord. I seldom saw any of these elegant beasts, bar an occasional sighting near the main roads to Vadsø or Kirkenes. Still, nearly everyone seemed to have a connection with reindeer in one form or another – eating them of course, but also curing their skins and making leggings, boots, and fur coats from them as required, or fashioning knife handles, spoons, etc. from reindeer horn, nowadays as a pastime but formerly out of necessity.

Karl and Marianne 'owned' a few reindeer forming part of the flock tended by Henrik Mathiesen, a neighbour from Burnes. They were not alone in that but I was never all that sure of the exact nature of the 'clientship' between them. It seemed to be a time for all hands to the pumps, however, as the time to gather in the reindeer approached in late January or early February. Day after day, the rate of progress in collecting disparate elements of the flock was a constant subject of conversation, aided and abetted by regular radio reports. Persuading these skittish beasts to join in the assembly was a tricky business, needing patience, skill, and cunning. As far as I could understand, it involved the creation of a giant moveable funnel of sacks strung on posts into which the reindeer were painstakingly channelled and eventually corralled.

A dozen or so Sámi reindeer owners and herders ranged eagle-eyed back and forth among the reindeer as they loped round and round in that graceful fashion of theirs, effortlessly adjusting course when collisions seemed otherwise inevitable. Usually, the herders were quick to identify their own animals by their earmarks, and lassoes were flung to rope them by the horns as they passed. Only now and again did they miss their mark or capture some other owner's reindeer by mistake. It was an all-action scene as the business of slaughtering was also in full swing along the inner perimeter of the enclosure. This was a bloody sight as beasts were wrestled onto their backs, swiftly stabbed in the neck with a curved knife, and slit down the belly without delay, their entrails spilling onto the snow and staining it red.

The weather was clear but extremely cold with a bitter easterly breeze that chilled me to the marrow. Almost everyone – men and women – apart from those actively engaged in the process wore full-length reindeer fur coats, leggings and boots. The bright red, blue, and yellow trimmings of the furs and leg bands of the onlookers and the blue tunics of the workers with their customary red, blue, and yellow stripes and fur leggings stretching from ankle to thigh and tasselled reindeer boots with their multicoloured ankle bindings stood out in stark contrast to the snow and the undulating mass of grey and white deer. I wore layers of ordinary outdoor clothing, as much as I could manage to swathe myself in, but my feet had turned to frozen blocks of ice by the time I gained the shelter of Thomas's car on the way home. I had made the mistake of allowing the soles of my reindeer boots to become damp in the trampled snow interior of the coffee tent and suffered the consequences. I never felt colder in my life.

The reindeer breathed forth a cloud of vapour into the frosty air as they circulated within the temporary palisade of poles with sacking strung between, and columns of steam rose steadily from growing piles of skins

'SEPARATION' OF THE REINDEER

and butchered meat and intestines. The entire operation was

lit by a weak winter sun before the light faded and all became enveloped in the gloaming. The 'separation' of the reindeer was conducted according to a set pattern with which all present bar me were well acquainted. It was a memorable experience.

Marianne's approaching 65th birthday early in March became the date by which I decided to time my departure from Nesseby. The news was greeted with consternation by Karl and Marianne and was no less palatable to Thomas and Elen Bertha and their children, all of whom had grown accustomed to having me around. Karl sought to forestall my plans by offering to help me acquire a plot of land nearby on which to build a home for myself, going so far as to point out the spot he had in mind.

Before the arrival of that fateful day, however, we had to engage with Marianne's birthday celebrations. In the Nordic world, such occasions are important enough in their own right, but there was an extra element of poignancy in this one because of my imminent departure. The Bombans, Marianne's blood relatives, an old Nesseby family with Finnish connections, were there in strength and, likewise, the Tana kinfolk from Alleknjarg and Polmak, not to mention many Burnes neighbours and other friends.

I had set up the Tandberg tape recorder in my bedroom and had left the door open in the hope of being able to record items of interest, in particular *yoiks* and the like. I was not disappointed, for songs and speeches and *yoiks* there were aplenty, including one extemporaneous *yoik* in which I figured as the focus of attention. It was performed by one of the Bombans, Louise, wife of the retired local postman known as *'Poasta Hánsa'* or 'John the Post', as one might say. 'My' *yoik* – a calque on 'John the Post's' own highly popular *yoik* (simply called *'Poasta Hánsa'*) – described my coming to Nesseby, mentioned the houseful of Lindseth girls and the regrettable fact that the last of these had but recently married before she and I could be matched, and lamented my impending departure.

There was no shortage of food and drink including a certain beverage from the Tana 'distillery' which became the cause of my downfall before the night was over. I remember little of the rest of that bibulous evening apart from my being found spreadeagled in the snow on the broad of my back whence I was raised by helping hands and safely deposited in bed.

I suffered the consequences next day, of course, with a sore stomach and aching head. Before my eyes, a reel of tape whirled uselessly on the machine in my bedroom having spun to the end of its course. I was pleased to note that during the night the microphone had been commandeered by a succession of eager party-goers who had *yoiked* merrily until they and the tape recorder eventually ran out of road.

The following evening I went to visit '*Dudd-áddjá*' who was champing at the bit for news of the party. I told him as much as I remembered, not neglecting to mention the baneful effect the Tana moonshine had had on me. I shouldn't have drunk that stuff, he said, because they put dynamite in it. No joke I thought, but he was quite serious, as I understood when he went on to say that the contents of shotgun cartridges were routinely emptied into the wash in order to increase the potency of the finished product.

I bet your stomach aches, he said, but I can cure you. With that he filled a glass of cold water from the bucket of melting ice that stood in the kitchen and ordered me to drink from it while he held the palm of his hand against my stomach. As I sipped the water, I felt an extraordinary heat radiating into me. I had reason to be grateful to Dudda for next day I was, as Granny Cassidy used to say, 'as right as the mail'.

In general I'd had reason to be grateful for my robust good health. Apart from the usual sniffs and colds during the course of my stay in Nesseby, I suffered no setbacks, broken bones, or debilitating illnesses of any sort. This was just as well as I had no health insurance cover. Though technically a British citizen (if only by conquest as I am fond of saying), I carried an Irish passport and was not eligible for treatment under the health treaty between the U.K. and Norway. Thankfully I did not need it, but in retrospect it had been foolhardy of me in the first instance to have embarked on my travels without first having considered the possibility that I might fall ill at some point.

Perhaps my healthy diet of fish – mainly cod, supplemented with salmon in summer, and occasionally herring and halibut at other times – may have had something to do with my staying healthy. I must have eaten cod five or six times a week and still like it. The cod was boiled and served with cod liver oil or melted butter as a sauce. I preferred the latter. Vegetables featured rarely enough except for sodden potatoes, boiled and often left to cool in their own water. Ugh!

I never tired of the cod which came out of the pot in great meaty chunks, only the choicest pieces being selected for consumption and the rest discarded. According to time-honoured tradition, fish was cut up and prepared for pot or pan by the man of the house and, in the case of cod, it reached the table only when all were seated and ready to eat and not a moment before. The best cod had a strongly soporific effect.

Fishing was the mainstay of local employment and the rich grounds of the Varanger fjord provided a good living for those involved in it. At intervals, all along the shore, the catch hung to dry from wooden fish racks standing high against the sky and every house had its quota of fish and meat preserved for domestic use in the great outdoor freezer of wintertime. Other lesser fish varieties were generally turned into fish balls. Salmon steaks fresh from the

LANDING FISH IN NESSEBY

fjord were a special treat in summer, as were lake fish caught in winter by fishing through holes made in the ice. I got to like the local custom of stripping off the salmon skin and toasting it on forks before the open fire until it grew crisp and crunchy.

I heard of a curious belief attached to halibut, one of the

most sought-after fish in the sea. On their way to the shore, the fishermen passed by a distinctively shaped rock which they would strike with their gloves in the belief that this would guarantee them good luck and, in particular, that halibut would be counted among the catch. In the same context I

FISHERMEN IN NESSEBY

also heard it said that, were an unmarried man to be one of the crew and halibut were caught, the crew's good luck would be put down to his having engaged in sexual congress shortly before putting to sea and he would then be teased unmercifully.

Meat dishes came in the form of reindeer, lamb, and mutton. Reindeer steaks and joints of reindeer meat were a special treat. Hunks of deep frozen reindeer meat from the outdoor freezer were pared in wafer-thin slices into a pot of melted butter where they cooked through instantly as they curled up in the extreme temperature. Marianne was a decent enough cook, but Elen Bertha's cooking was on another plane altogether, as was widely acknowledged by all who knew her. Elen Bertha told me that eating reindeer tongue – especially the tip of the tongue – would make me '*gielis*' i.e. turn me into a liar.

Once, I entered her kitchen just as she was removing a loaf of bread from the oven and, for some perverse reason or other, I got the whiff, not of fresh bread but of bacon and eggs, that brought me straight back to Ireland and set me longing for a 'fry'. Bacon there was to be had, of course, but it was an insipid and undistinguished product by comparison with its Irish counterpart. Finnish bacon was particularly prized because of its inordinately high fat content and the older generation set extra store on it because of that.

The quality of reindeer carcasses was also judged by the

depth of fat they carried. I once heard a reindeer carcase described in exactly the same terms applied to Mac Dathó's famous pig in the old Irish saga *Scéla Mucce Meic Dathó*, namely sporting a layer of fat to the depth of 'four fingers and a thumb standing up'. Some, like Karl, would only eat the fattest part of the meat, systematically cutting away the lean which they called *'čáhppes biergu'*, literally 'black meat'.

The year I spent in Norwegian Lapland left a deep impression on me. I had been remarkably fortunate in many respects in finding a family and a community that accepted me in their midst, a stranger from a distant island in the Atlantic whose interests they indulged and smiled upon, though no doubt simultaneously baffled to a degree as to why anyone should take the bother of learning a language then viewed more and more as fast becoming redundant to requirements. An opinion I heard voiced more than once was: *'It sámegielain birge guhkkelii go Ceavccegeađgái'* – 'You won't manage with the Sámi language farther than Ceavccegeađge' (a nearby settlement – 'Mortensnes' in Norwegian – on the road to Vadsø).

Prejudice there was aplenty too, fuelled in large measure over generations by the naked opposition of the Norwegian state to Sámi language and culture. Policy in this regard had begun to shift more or less as I arrived and a more enlightened view towards Sámi language and culture gradually emerged. The Lindseth children, for example, were able to avail of a couple of hours of school instruction in their home language where nothing of the kind previously existed. Within a short number of years, all-Sámi kindergartens and schools were established and young mothers were granted paid leave of absence and childcare facilities while learning to read and write their home language.

Ingrained notions of superiority obtained among sections of the non-Sámi population, some of which I witnessed at first hand as in Vadsø, for example, where I once heard a gang of youths and urchins hurling insults at a man clad in Sámi costume *'Lapp djevel'* – 'Lappish devil' – they cried as they followed after him along the street. Truth to tell, those idiots probably had a fair dollop of Sámi and/or Kvaen blood in them. Karl and Marianne's youngest daughter, Aud, lived on the island of Vardø (a mainly Norwegian-speaking community) where her few Sámi acquaintances among the population avoided speaking to her in Sámi language in case the Vardø folk would realise they were Sámis.

Years later Ellen Lindseth told me of the cruel rebuff she received from her office colleagues (also in Vadsø) when, shortly after taking up employment there, she innocently suggested that she turn up at a fancy-dress party in her Sámi regalia. '*Gjør ikke det, gjør ikke det!*' they chorused – 'Not that, oh, not that!' By and large, however, it is only fair to say that overt anti-Sámi discrimination was not a dominant feature of life there; at least it did not seem to impinge to any significant extent on people's daily lives except in the field of education. It was in the air, nevertheless, redolent to some extent of the sort of sentiment expressed by Hans Kristian Adamson and Per Klein in their book *Blood on the Midnight Sun* (New York, 1964, pp. 228-9) in respect of a hated traitor of the Nazi Occupation period called Henry Oliver Rinnan (also known as 'The Devil's Apprentice'):

> In addition to being unusually undersized in a land of brawny men, he had coarse black hair and piercing eyes with a faint slant. This, together with his narrow face and high cheek bones, combined to give Rinnan's features a distinctly oriental cast. There was about him something that suggested a throwback to the 'Small People' – called Samers [Sámis] – who invaded Norway from Siberia many centuries ago. They were dark and mysterious nomads whose penetrating eyes seemed to hypnotize and whose hearts were cold and cruel. They were endowed with primitive animal cunning and their souls – so the Nordmen of the Middle Ages believed – had been sold to the Devil. In return they had received supernatural knowledge of human nature as well as clairvoyant and telepathic powers. It would seem that all of these qualities had been bestowed on Rinnan ... there was nothing in Rinnan's appearance to point to his Norwegian ancestry.

*   *   *

I have never forgotten the friends I made there who, without fuss or formality, introduced me to their language and culture, permitted me to become a member of their community, and shared their lives with me. Contact has been maintained and those friendships have endured over the decades that have elapsed since then, interrupted by the passing of many of the people who once made me welcome among them, but also strengthened and renewed by intermittent visits to Ireland by descendants of the old couple I lived with, and by others, and also by my return visits to my old stomping grounds.

Marianne and Karl, Thomas and Elen Bertha, the Burnes neighbours, and assorted denizens of Nesseby (including, of course, Siri and Olav Dikkanen who in a sense had made it all possible),  Thomas & Elen Bertha Lindseth and the friends in Tana, far too numerous to mention, made me one of their own and I will never forget them for it. All good and kindly people, most of them, alas, now gone to their reward.

Some weeks later, I embarked on the long bus and train journey south to Stockholm *en route* to Germany. Curiously, I remember hardly anything of my round of farewells other than Marianne's distress at losing her *biebmogánda* ('foster-son'). She asked in her soft-voiced, shy way if she should send me *Finnmarken*, the local paper, perhaps in emulation of my mother's faithful weekly despatch of Saturday's *Irish Times* to me all the time I was in Nesseby. Marianne and Karl were a good-natured, generous, and caring couple who contributed in no small way to the success of my stay among the Sámi people of Varanger. We had come a long way together since our first awkward encounter and it was a painful parting for both parties.

I left them behind with a heavy heart, only consoled by the knowledge that I carried away with me a first-hand understanding of their home language and culture as well as a smattering of other vernaculars, a bundle of notebooks chock-a-bloc with various scribblings, and a collection of valuable audio-recordings, slides, and photographs.

Heinrich's gesture in dispensing with my services as his research assistant by equating the discharge of my duties in that respect with a licence to roam and research abroad was unconventional and absolutely typical of the man. As far as he was concerned, my peregrinations paid off when I returned with a good knowledge of the dialect of the Sámi language we had studied together before my departure for Lapland, together with an insight into different aspects of Sámi folk tradition and culture as a result of my collecting efforts in Nesseby and Tana.

I knew Heinrich would be pleased and looked forward to meeting him in Germany. Mission accomplished!

Going Home

B Y NOW I was an old hand at trekking up and down the lesser known reaches of Scandinavia and Finland. While stopping in Stockholm, I made a short visit to Uppsala, a university town, an hour to the north. I had consulted with the Irish embassy about the Celtic lecturership there. The current incumbent was Seán de Búrca, whose appointment was temporary, and he introduced me to the staff member in charge of the position at the time, acting Professor of Folklore, Bo Almquist. Bo confirmed that there was an upcoming vacancy, of which he would notify me. My acquaintance with Bo would last for forty-five years until his death in 2013.

That same day, I *almost* met another person whose life and mine became intertwined subsequently, namely Maj Magnusson, my wife and life-time partner. She studied Folklore with Bo in Uppsala and was also one of Seán de Burca's Irish language students, and locked in conclave with him that day just a few doors away while Bo and I chatted.

From Stockholm, I went to Bonn to learn German, travelling by train via Malmö and Hamburg with the novelty of a roll-on-roll-off train ferry in between. Heinrich advised that a German Celticist of his acquaintance by the name of Rolf Baumgarten had consented to be of assistance to me. I found Rolf at the *Sprachwißenschaftliches Institut der Universität Bonn* which housed the Celtic Studies centre. With Rolf's help, I found a place to stay, a single room in a family home in Herwarthstraße. For a small fee, I enrolled as an occasional student at the university and thus became entitled to attend a German language course for foreigners there, and enrolled for a course in *Sitte und Brauch* ('Custom and Usage') given by the Professor of Ethnology (*Volkskunde*), Matthias Zender.

Through Rolf's good offices I secured a study base at the Institute where, after a year in the wilderness, I found myself surrounded by books. I was introduced to Johann Knobloch, one of the professors there, and in due course invited to attend his fortnightly seminar. A man called Heinrich Becker was also in attendance and never missed an opportunity to talk in Irish with me.

BONN UNIVERSITY

Becker had been stranded in Ireland at the outbreak of war in 1939 and had spent much of his time in the Aran Islands where he had perfected his knowledge of Irish and made substantial collections of folklore and took many excellent photographs. Inevitably, he was believed by some to have been a Nazi spy. I also heard it said that there was a touch of 'brown' i.e. Nazi about Professor Knobloch, but, perhaps, few Germans (or Austrians as he was) of that generation could escape stories of that kind about them cropping up. He was a friendly sort and helpful to me at all times, even to the extent of insisting on speaking German to me when it would have been much easier for him to use English. Before leaving Bonn, my German had improved to the point where I was able to successfully manage a reasonable conversation with him in that language.

The Institute was a godsend in other ways on Saturdays when Rolf and I would have recourse to its deserted kitchen facilities to brew coffee as an accompaniment to the lunches – mainly *frikadellen* (meatball) sandwiches, *rollmops* (pickled herring), and cream buns – we purchased in a nearby delikatessen. On weekdays, the Student Union 'Mensa', where one could eat substantial if not particularly palatable meals at the cost of one Mark, was of necessity a favourite resort, while on Sundays we often had recourse to a Turkish café where

I once abstracted a large rubber band from the heart of my half-eaten burger.

I also took some classes in Hungarian from a man whose first name I never knew but who went by the designation Dr von László. He was an émigré of the old school, very formal in manner and antedeluvian in his didactic approach. I liked him for all that and, being his only student, I somehow got the impression that he was depending on my not giving up on him as he would then have no students at all and thereby suffer pecuniary loss.

Our weekly proceedings were conducted in a mixture of German and English (of which he had a smattering), and a textbook entitled *Einführung in das Ungarische* was the instrument of torture used. It was an East German production, printed on something closely resembling downmarket toilet paper and full of turgid prose passages lauding the kind of achievements dear to Communist hearts – tractor plants and parts, collective farming and five-year agricultural plans, friendship pacts, workers' solidarity and the like.

Dr von László would analyse the grammar of one of these passages, go through the vocabulary, then read the text aloud and have me repeat it after him until he was satisfied that I had got the pronunciation exactly right. That was the easy bit, for between lessons I then had to learn this text off by heart and regurgitate it word for word for him next time around. I adhered faithfully to this routine and got my reward at the end of our last lesson when he stood up and, formally shaking hands with me, declared in heavily accented English – 'I thank you for your very interesting!' I waited for the rest of the sentence, but that was it. We said our farewells and never saw each other again.

I remember little of the Marxist-Leninist guff (which was probably no more to Dr von László's liking than it was to mine) and all that has stuck in my mind from all of that are a few polite words and phrases and one perfectly valid but stunningly useless sentence that runs the famous 'Lo! The postillion has been hit by lightning!' close. It goes like this: „*A Magyar zászló piros fehér zöld*" meaning 'The Hungarian flag is red, white, and green'. The only remarkable thing about this conversation-stopper is that it is a prime example of a nominal sentence i.e. a sentence with no verb since, word for word, it simply states 'The Hungarian flag red white green.'

Bonn was the capital of West Germany in those days, of course, and there were embassies galore in and around the suburbs and in places like Bad Godesberg where the Irish Embassy was located. The ambassador of the day was a decent man called Eamonn Kennedy with whom I had dealings of a most unusual

BONN IN THE 1960s

nature arising from the unfortunate loss of a substantial portion of the haul of tapes and photos I had carried with me from Lapland.

One Friday evening, some time after my arrival in Bonn, I met up with Rolf in the Institute where he had arranged access to the audiovisual facilities in order to view my slides and sample some of the recordings I had made. We spent some pleasant hours together there and, in due course, found ourselves in the Münsterplatz, in a pub called *Gaststätte „Hähnchen"* ('The Cockerel'), where we had some pub grub and a glass or two of Kölsch, one of the local beers.

Next morning, I awoke in Herwarthstraße to the devastating realization that I had left the large plastic bag holding my Lapland treasure under the table in the pub. I hurried back to the *„Hähnchen"* as quickly as my legs would carry me but could find no trace of the bag or its contents. My bumbling enquiries drew little response of any kind from management and I was forced to rouse Rolf from his slumbers to come to my aid, which he did with alacrity. We were told that nobody had seen hide nor hair of the plastic bag in question and that all the detritus from the previous evening's eating and drinking had been dumped already. They said we were welcome to inspect the rubbish bins if we wished.

So it was that Rolf and I found ourselves digging for gold, bare-armed and elbow-deep, in the nauseating mess of pub-leavings of the night before. We were rewarded with the emergence of a few tapes and boxes of slides from the food and other waste, representing but a fraction of what had disappeared. We quickly formed the opinion that there might be more elsewhere,

MÜNSTERPLATZ, BONN, 1968

but the manager was adamant that nothing of interest had been found in the pub, despite the evidence that at least some of the contents of the missing bag had somehow made their way into the rubbish bins and, we concluded, had hardly done so unaided.

Desperate times require desperate measures and, at that point, I concluded that I had no option but to seek the assistance of the Ambassador in the rescue effort. I got the number of his residence and rang him there. My tale of woe must have sounded improbable – an extended field trip to Lapland, a visit to Germany on the way home to Ireland, a night out with a few drinks, a rude awakening next morning, a desperate rummage through bins of trash and, finally, dark suspicions that the management of the pub, despite their protestations to the contrary, did know more than they were prepared to admit about the missing items. For whatever reason, my entreaties were successful and resulted in his relinquishing his Saturday morning leisure and motoring to my rescue in the Münsterplatz.

In the meantime, Rolf and I relayed the news to all and sundry that the Ambassador was on his way to investigate the matter. Sure enough, the owner emerged from the *Gaststätte* a short time after, bearing an armful of missing tapes which he said he had discovered in his son's living quarters. This development coincided more or less with the appearance of His Excellency who witnessed this denouement with some degree of satisfaction. He was, indeed, a most excellent Excellency!

Some of my precious store remained missing and gone forever. It goes without saying that the son of the house responsible for this depredation had no interest in the contents of my tapes but rather coveted the actual tapes themselves which he intended to re-use for making his own recordings. Perhaps this process had already begun by the time I discovered my loss, but there is no gainsaying the fact that none of this would have happened had I been more careful with my possessions in the first place.

I had entered Germany as a tourist and as such was permitted a three-month stay without further formality. Somewhere along the line, someone mentioned to me that it might be a good idea for me to register with the police, just in case I was run over by a bus or otherwise suffered accidental injury. This, I was told, could result in appalling difficulties of an unspecified nature with the powers that be. So it transpired that with Rolf, as ever, at my elbow, I presented myself for registration at the relevant office. The official with whom I was dealing became highly agitated, shouting, waving his arms and banging the counter in front of me. I was to depart at once, he said, under pain of I cannot remember what. In the end, Rolf's patient negotiation on my behalf earned me a stay of execution, and I was able to remain in situ for a further three or four weeks. Documents were produced, signed and countersigned, and emphatically stamped in triplicate and, eventually, I was dismissed with great bad grace, let loose to do my worst on the German population at large in the little time remaining to me.

My unpleasant duty was then to inform my landlord and

his mother that I would be forced by circumstances beyond my control to vacate my room and its six-month lease and leave for home. They were not best pleased to say the least and made no secret of their disapproval of me. In fairness to them, however, when I said my farewells, they wished me *bon voyage* and presented me with a bottle of choice Mosel wine.

My next task was to arrange for my passage home and this I managed to do by cashing in my open return air ticket London-Stockholm, which was still valid because of the terms on which it had been purchased. I was granted a refund amounting to £70 or so, more than enough to cover my train fare from Bonn to Ostend in Belgium where I would catch a ferry across the Channel to Dover and then a train to London. I also booked a train ticket from London (Euston) to Heysham and a first-class ticket on the Heysham to Belfast steamer.

HEYSHAM TO BELFAST FERRY, 1960S

My departure from Bonn railway station was on a Saturday towards the end of July 1968. That morning, accompanied by Rolf and other friends, I had visited the fruit market in the Römerplatz to purchase fruit for the journey and stood with them for a while on the platform when a familiar figure came limping into sight, none other than Johann Knobloch accompanied by his wife. He had come to say farewell and presented me with a handsome little volume of German folk music and song as a going-away present. His wife, whom I had never met before, handed over a huge bag of fruit for the journey! Laden to the ground with fruit and all my other bits and pieces, I thanked them one and all, waved goodbye to them and to Bonn.

*   *   *

The long train journey across north-western Germany via Aachen, across the border and on to Ostend (from where I would board the ferry to Dover) seemed to take forever. Earlier, I had written to my sister, Sheila, then nursing in Northampton, mentioning a date and a place when we might meet in London. I did not know London at all and picked Piccadilly Circus as a possible rendezvous for no particular reason other than it was a well-known landmark and place I had heard of and, I guessed, she had too.

I spent a fruitless couple of hours at Piccadilly waiting for my sister who never showed up. I heard later that my letter had been delivered to the house next door by mistake and that she did not receive it until I was long gone from the scene and back in Ireland. I took the tube to Euston and, as I perused a wall map of tangled tube lines, I heard some staccato accents, unmistakably Belfast, behind me. It was a bunch of young men en route to Euston on the same mission as myself and equally anxious not to lose their way.

I sauntered and they jogged along, but I kept catching up with them at regular intervals as they halted to study wall maps, chattering and gesticulating the while. Eventually, we fetched up at the right station and stood within earshot of one another on the platform. They continued to speculate as to whether or not they had successfully navigated the maze, and they decided to ask someone. I braced myself for the encounter, but their emissary walked by me and straight up to a quintessential London gent in full ceremonial uniform – pin-stripe trousers, rolled umbrella and bowler hat. The Belfast lad shot his question at him minus preliminaries of any sort – 'How do you get from Piccadilly to Euston?' said he. The gent stared at him blankly as this question was repeated over and over again, drawing no response whatsoever from him. The lad returned to his friends waiting all agog to hear how he got on. 'See him,' said the lad without a blush, 'I couldn't understand a word he said!' I could have hugged him. With that the train arrived and we all clambered aboard and all ended happily.

Weighed down with baggage, I struggled up and down the corridor of the Euston to Heysham train in a seemingly fruitless search for a seat, when a friendly voice hailed me from within an already crowded compartment, intimating a solution to my predicament. Two hefty fellows hoisted my baggage onto the rack and others engineered a place for me to sit. Their posture and haircuts were a giveaway and their accents – a mélange of dialects – revealed Irish origins. I was right on both scores for they turned out to be Irish Guards in mufti, all headed home on leave.

They were a chatty lot and one fellow in particular was relentless in his pursuit of information about me and my travels. I told him I had been in Germany. He replied that he had served there, mentioning some army camp or other, and wanted to know where I had been. I told him I had been at the university in Bonn. The inevitable follow-up question left me in a quandary as he wanted to know what I studied there and I was unsure what I should say. Eventually, I settled on 'Celtic Studies', at which point a strange silence descended upon the company. This was broken by my interrogator's baffling non sequitur – 'That's where it started, wasn't it, Luther and all that!' It took a moment or two for me to realize that he had understood me to say 'Catholic' rather than 'Celtic', names that do not sound altogether dissimilar in Belfast argot. We quickly sorted things out, though I do not think any of them were much the wiser for my explanation as to what I really had been up to. We shared the last of my fruit among us and engaged in genial conversation until we parted company on the quay.

I had booked first-class in anticipation of needing a good rest after the journey and set a course straight for the appropriate gangplank. The officer in charge was visibly surprised when I produced my first-class ticket, having pointed immediately in the direction of second-class when he first caught sight of me. It was a good crossing and I felt refreshed as I took my first breath of Irish air in many a long month early next day.

It was a fine morning, and as I had a couple of hours and

more until I caught a bus for Omagh, I decided to head in the direction of Queen's and to call on my former landlady, Bridget Kelly, in Camden Street. There were no buses running as far as I could see, so I walked, baggage and all. It felt good to be on home soil and I looked all around me as I meandered up Great Victoria Street. Off to my right in the direction of the Loyalist enclave of Sandy Row, my eye fell on a proclamation painted on a gable wall that gave me pause: 'We are the people,' it announced to the world. I trudged along, put on notice that I had somehow been consigned to some sub-human category, a feeling I had not experienced since leaving home. My Sámi and German friends would not have approved. Nothing had changed in my absence. A qualified welcome home, then. Yip, it was nice to be back ... up to a point.

BACK IN BELFAST

My father had wanted to fetch me from Belfast, but I must have felt reluctant to call my vagabond existence over until I reached Tyrone and so it was that the less-than-salubrious surroundings of Omagh Bus Station marked the termination of my odyssey and reabsorption into the bosom of my family, for the time being at least.

Family, Roots & Music

THREE PARISHES belonging to the Diocese of Clogher – Dromore, Ederney, and Termonmagrath – hold Langfield in their embrace. The northern end of the parish of Dromore stretches to within just a few miles of Drumquin at the Pigeon Top, a mountainy height in the townland of Aughadulla. In bygone times, this eminence enjoyed a certain notoriety as an age-old landmark marked on medieval maps as *Sliabh Learga*, where it stood sentinel as the last northern outpost of Clogher. Northwards across the lower reaches of Langfield *Sliabh Learga* faces Baronscourt, seat of the Duke of Abercorn, and its sister peak, *Sliabh Troim*, mentioned in the *Annals of the Four Masters*, but renamed in Plantation times as Bessy Bell.

The diocesan frontier falls away steeply to the southwest revealing magnificent views across Lower Lough Erne to the distant hills of Fermanagh. At this point, the high ground between Fermanagh and Tyrone constitutes a watershed between the Erne and Foyle basins. As an old friend of mine, Michael McCanny (Mickey Neilly), a resident of those parts, had it, your water would go by the Foyle or the Erne depending on which door you might exit to answer a call of nature when playing cards or *céilí*-ing in one of the local houses.

Similarly, from the rising ground on the northern limits of Langfield, the wide expanse of County Donegal comes into view. The scene is punctuated at intervals by a succession of distinctively shaped mountain tops. The quartzite cone of Errigal – Donegal's highest peak at 751 metres – guards the entrance to the Rosses in the far northwest; hump-backed Muckish lies to its east, and due north of us lies 'Dark Inishowen'. From there too you can follow the line of the

Finn Valley west to Altnapaste and the Blue Stack Mountains behind whose southern escarpment, in the lee of *An Chruach Ghorm* (the Blue Stack itself), lies a hidden valley known as 'The Croaghs' or *'Na Cruacha'* to give it its true Irish name.

With spectacular scenery of such a high order beckoning in almost every direction, it was small wonder that natives of Langfield sometimes neglected to appreciate the attractions of their home ground which was generally perceived as being rather ordinary by comparison with the outstanding beauty on the doorstep. Felix Kearney (1888-1977) did his best to bring home its charms to us in a well-beloved song of his making called 'The Hills above Drumquin' which also gained popularity in places far removed from Langfield. It is set to the air of 'She lived beside the Anner' and contains the following lines which many Langfield people occasionally find quoted at them in unexpected places:

> Drumquin you're not a city but you're all the world to me,
> Your lot I'll never pity should you never greater be.

Some of these sentiments may have been inspired by no less a personage than Colm Cille himself, that irascible Donegal man who for all his bad temper became the famous saint of Derry and Iona. According to Paddy McAleer, a one-time neighbour of mine, during a visit paid by Colm Cille to Drumquin, the wily natives milked his goat unnoticed by him whereupon, as Paddy put it, 'he went up the Cow Market, looked down the town and cried out – "There you are Drumquin, you'll never be any better!" ' A story of more or less the same ilk is reported from Skerries, north County Dublin, where it is said the natives committed the even more heinous offence of finishing off Saint Patrick's goat entirely, killing and then eating it, thus earning themselves the soubriquet 'The Skerries Goats'.

JOHN O'KANE

My father, John, had three brothers, Jim, Pat, and Francis, and two sisters, Catherine and Alice, all born in Dooish,

County Tyrone, but only Jim, Pat, and my father grew to manhood, the girls and his brother Francis falling victims to the 'Spanish Flu' of 1918, all three succumbing within a few weeks of one another, leaving my grandparents desolate. Granny O'Kane was distraught and rendered incapable of registering much of what was going on around her, so much so that a local woman who worked for her quietly took away the dead children's clothes, item by item; and in the course of the following year she turned them into a beautiful quilt, which she gave to her. Granny gave it to my mother, and my brother Seán and his wife Ella are its custodians today. My father's brother, Jim, was able to identify many of the individual pieces as having once been worn by this or that child.

JAMES O'KANE

ALICE O'KANE
NÉE GALLAGHER

My Uncle Jim grew up to be what was known as a tangler, having inherited a small farm in Corraheskin, hard by Cornavarra, but located just within the confines of the neighbouring parish of Dromore. He led a colourful life, attending cattle fairs all over west Ulster and north Connacht, where he exercised his skill to the full in buying beasts on an empty pocket and selling them on later at the same fair at a better price, thus enabling him to pay off the debt incurred at the outset and earn a small profit. This was nerve-wracking stuff, for sometimes things did not work out as planned and he would be forced to abandon all and make a speedy exit. His special expertise, however, lay in buying sheep in the hills of west Donegal and running them across the border. He had a wry sense of humour and was a noted raconteur. He and his wife Mary had no family. Jim survived her, lived to be 91, and in later years his home became a *céilí*-ing house where neighbours gathered to discuss the affairs of the world including the various intricacies of EU agricultural policies.

My father's youngest brother Pat was also my godfather.

Rather late in life, he married a local schoolteacher, my first teacher, indeed, and a distant member of the wider O'Kane clan from the neighbouring parish of Dregish. Una and he adopted four children. Pat, a teetotaller, with not an ounce of humour in his body, placed an inordinate emphasis on piety and religious observance, and much to everyone's dissatisfaction became the self-appointed guardian of the morals of his brother's children, myself and my five siblings, Sheila, Seán, Aidan, Brendan, and Declan. He and Jim were as different as chalk and cheese and appeared to have little time for one another.

My mother Teresa (1917-1996) was also a member of a big family, all girls but for the eldest and youngest, James and Patrick. In between, there was Annie, Bridget (Bea), Kathleen (Cassie), Margaret (Cissie), Tessie, Rose (Dean), and Susie. She was raised in Glengesh, and in the Barr, parish of Fintona, across the county march, then briefly in Fintona itself and, latterly, in

Teresa O'Kane
née Cassidy

the town of Omagh. Her father, James Cassidy (1874-1966), a native of Glengesh in the parish of Pubble (or Tempo), County Fermanagh, worked the family farm in Glengesh and later another farm in the adjacent townland of the Barr, a tidy holding of some 100 acres including a sizeable chunk of mountain, all of which he subsequently sold for a pittance.

He was a reluctant and rather inefficient farmer at best by all accounts, on one occasion, it is said, having sown broad beans by simply broadcasting rather than planting them. But he excelled in other ways being a joiner by trade and a skilful

James Cassidy

one too. He had served his time to the trade in Scotland where he led a penurious existence as an apprentice, so much so that he was forced to give up milk in his tea in order to save money. He drank black tea all his life as a result. To distinguish them from the many other Cassidy females of that place, his many daughters were known as 'the Joiner's cutties' ('cutty' being the common word for a 'girl'). He had two sons, James who died in infancy and many years later, Patrick, the last of the brood who grew into a dashing young fellow with a fine singing voice, an eye for the ladies, and a taste for the drink. Perhaps, the arrival of a seemingly unending succession of female children played a part in encouraging Granda Cassidy to withdraw from farming life at an early stage as he faced into a future without the prospect of the kind of help a man like him with a limited interest in working the land needed.

My mother's mother was Bridget Slevin (1884-1966) from Dromore Lower in the parish of Eskra (formerly Clogher), hard by Kilnahushoge where the celebrated nineteenth-century Tyrone author, William Carleton, once went to school. By the time she married James Cassidy, many of her siblings – her brother Johnny, and sisters Anne, Teresa, Rose, and Susan – had taken the emigrant boat to America. On Bridget's marriage and that of her other sisters, Brian Slevin and his wife Anne were left with an empty house bar Granny's bachelor brother Brian.

BRIDGET CASSIDY
NÉE SLEVIN

⸌ My father was a good dancer and loved music but did not play or sing. Much like the Gallaghers on my father's side, the Slevins of Dromore Lower were also a musical bunch. My maternal grandmother, Bridget, played the fiddle and melodeon and, on occasion, my mother the fiddle.

Bridget Slevin called her daughters after her sisters, my mother included. My mother's Aunt Tessie left for America aged 18 in 1911 and never returned, though one of her children did so many years later. His name was Frank Kumagai and he was half Japanese. Like his mother and her husband, he had been interned in the Land of the Free during the Second World War. The Slevin girls were noted dancers who practised their routine on the concrete platform between the cows in the byre, their arms resting on a beast on either side thus freeing up their feet to tap out the steps. Invariably, they were called upon 'to open the ball' at house dances in the locality.

Their mother, Anne McGirr, was the daughter of another Cassidy from Glengesh. Because of this, the issue of consanguinity arose briefly before the all clear was given for Granny Cassidy to marry her Glengesh Cassidy. They met at the fair of Fintona, more or less halfway between their respective homesteads. She had gone to a fortune-teller that day who told her that she was destined to meet her future husband soon, that he would be tall, dark, and handsome and that he would, as she put it, 'come in like a lion and go out like a lamb.' In other words, he'd have a short temper. My mother told me that her father, when something went awry while he was working at his trade, would fling from him in frustration the hammer or whatever tool he happened to have in hand with total disregard as to where it might land or whom it might strike. My late brother, Brendan, inherited some of the irascible genes and could fly into a temper in exactly the same way as our Granda Cassidy.

*   *   *

A constant in my life has been music and song, a love of which I did not take off the grass, as they say. Both my grannies played: Bridget Slevin, the fiddle and the melodeon, and Alice Gallagher, the fiddle.

Liza Alice Cassidy of Glengesh in the parish of Pubble, County Fermanagh, was a step-dancer and singer, and her descendants were also adept at the art. It must have been pleasing to her grand-daughter, Bridget, that she should take up residence in Glengesh when she married James Cassidy, a member of one of the many Cassidy families in that place.

After the death of her husband James Cassidy, my Granny Bridget, lived with us in Drumquin and at one point elected to buy herself a melodeon. Her fingers stiff with age let her down however and, much to her disgust, she found that she was only able to pick out the simplest of tunes. She loved to hear us children play and sing.

My mother Teresa, or 'Tessie', received an unusual wedding present in the shape of a five-string banjo on which we as children drummed relentlessly but never played, except my brother, Aidan, who was destined to inherit this instrument in due course. Tessie must have had notions of becoming a banjo-player herself at some stage, but she never advanced beyond a few tunes on the fiddle, her party piece being 'Danny Boy'.

Some of us were sent to learn the piano and violin with Miss McCullagh of John Street in Omagh. She was a strict disciplinarian and an excellent teacher who wielded a mean ruler with which she administered many a sharp rap on the knuckles. My mother made us practise hard and we did well in music examinations. To her great pride, one year my youngest brother, Declan, walked off with a prestigious prize at Derry *Feis*, beating 'the Derry ones' – a city famous for music – into a cocked hat.

SÉAMAS & DECLAN

My father, Johnny, was known as 'Big Johnny' to distinguish him from other 'John O'Kanes' of the locality (one of whom rejoiced in the felicitous nickname of 'The Smiler', a soubriquet borne to the present day by his descendants called as a group 'The Smilers').

For all his bulk, my father was a nifty dancer, well practised in the popular steps of Highlands, Mazurkas, Polkas, Two-steps, Barn Dances, and the like. He loved music and song but like every man-jack of the O'Kanes of Langfield had no singing voice. My brother, Seán and my sister, Sheila, emulated him in both respects, having inherited his terpsichorean genes coupled with his lack of a singing voice. Otherwise, the only deviants from the O'Kane norm were myself (accordion) and three younger siblings – Aidan (banjo), Brendan (guitar), and Declan (fiddle) – and we all sang.

I was dragooned into learning Irish dancing but, unlike my sister Sheila, was never much good at it. What I lacked in finesse I made up for in commitment and determination at least to judge by my performance one summer Sunday at Tattysallagh sports; urged to give it my best shot, with one giant leap I sailed high in the air clear of the platform and into the crowd ranged about.

There was never any shortage of music and song at the many Christmas parties held in our family home at which pretty well the entire extended family would assemble. All were expected to contribute in some way to the proceedings, usually in the form of a party piece, a song or recitation or story of some sort, ready for delivery at the appropriate moment, and some came armed with instruments.

TERESA O'KANE

The men who married 'the Joiner's cutties' always contributed. Dan McGrath from Arvalee, near Omagh, would sing of the famous greyhound 'Master McGrath'; Tommy Fullan from Portadown would highlight the sectarian ambience of his neck of the woods with 'The Oul' Orange Flute'; John McCrossan of Drumquin sang of 'The Rose of Tralee' in faraway Kerry (where his sister was married); and Packie O'Hagan of Eskra played the fiddle.

The 'Joiner's cutties' themselves also contributed: my Aunt Kathleen would always sing 'When the Fields are White with Daisies' and her younger sisters, Susie and Dean (Rose) were sure to come up with some popular ditty of the day by the likes of Delia Murphy, Gracie Fields, Doris Day, or Jo Stafford; my mother would play 'Danny Boy', and all would join in. Pat, the Joiner's 'cub', sang in fine voice Percy French's 'The Pride of Petravore'. Dance music was supplied by the gramophone, Jimmy Shand and his band and The Gallowglass Céilí Band being among the favourites.

Featured among the recitations were Robert Service's 'Dangerous Dan McGrew' by Dan McGrath, and my sister

Sheila's rendition of 'The Will' by local poet, Felix Kearney, and my father would act out a story about an unfortunate individual with pockets full of eggs that ended in his unwittingly slapping his hands against his thighs with predictable results. Elizabeth Shane's 'Wee Hughie' (full of dialect words) was another favourite recitation in which all joined in – 'He's gone to school, Wee Hughie, and him not four...'

In the days before the venue shifted to Drumquin, these Christmas parties were held at the home of my mother's parents, James and Bridget Cassidy, in Fairmount Avenue, Omagh, where, as in Drumquin, all ate and drank of the best Christmas fare and rejoiced in each other's company, as did the many cousins assembled together from all over West Tyrone on these occasions.

From time to time, parties were held in other houses belonging to the extended family and in private houses elsewhere in the parish. I remember parties like this in Coll's of Claramore, in O'Kane's of Legphreshy, and in Willie Gorman's tiny cottage in Tully, and also a number of events in Kelly's of Deroran where my Aunt Kathleen and her husband Paddy presided over the proceedings.

At one of these, Paddy handed my father and me bumpers of whiskey apiece on entry. Barely out of my teens, I wondered for a moment what to do with mine, when, quick as a flash Paddy remarked with a twinkle in his eye – 'There, Séamas, make a spoon or spoil a horn!' This exhortation (referring to the old custom of carving spoons from horn, a process that required a highly delicate approach to shaping the finished product which could easily be holed and rendered useless by an injudicious flick of the carving knife) defused what might have been an awkward situation and all was well. I took it to mean – I was to enjoy my whiskey carefully, but not make a fool of myself!

In time, my brothers, Aidan, Brendan, and Declan became experienced stage musicians with various local groups such as 'The Candy Style', a country music band, and 'Knotty Pine', a Bluegrass music outfit that has achieved national prominence in Bluegrass circles. Most important and most enjoyable for all of us were the times we got to play and sing together at family gatherings, birthdays, weddings, wedding anniversaries and the like.

AIDAN, SEÁN, BRENDAN, DECLAN, SHEILA & SÉAMAS, IN 2010

Once, at a cousin's wedding, we took the stage and played a few tunes while the band that had been specially hired for the occasion took a break. We must not have done too badly for the review of the wedding video by the groom and his people was said to have drawn comments to the effect that hiring not one but two bands was a totally unnecessary extravagance!

The tradition is actively carried on by the younger members of the family – Declan's sons, Neil and Colin, who are accomplished guitarists and singers, Aidan's sons, Ciarán and Diarmuid who play the fiddle and guitar, and my daughter, Sorcha, who also plays the fiddle as well as the tin whistle,

SORCHA AND PÁDRAIG

guitar, and bodhrán, and who has a beautiful singing voice.

*   *   *

My mother's oldest sister, Annie, gave me this account of my grandmother's people:

'Well, I think she was the most marvellous singer, "Granny Cassidy" – my mother. Her and Minnie used to sing together and she played the fiddle. Her mother was great too and her mother before her, Liza Alice Cassidy. She was famous. She sung "The Parting Glass".

'There was one time there was a Fair Day in Tempo and somebody sang Liza Alice's – my grandmother's – song "The Parting Glass". And this man hit the counter and he says: "I never heard anybody ever could sing that song like Liza Alice Cassidy!"

'She [Lisa Alice Cassidy] was a step-dancer too. She was tall and light and a great dancer and a great singer, great. She was reared in Glengesh and I suppose they were all step-dancers at that time. Somebody learned her and she was marvellous. She used to open the ball, you know, every year for the Mason's [McGirrs], herself and another man. She used to take off her shoes and that was the first dance that was danced, her and some neighbour man that was a good dancer. She was the loveliest singer ever opened a mouth and she died very young. She was only a young woman when she died. Her mother again was a good singer too. It was handed down.'

Granny Cassidy, lived with us in the end of her days and I wondered when she once heard me sing that song why she immediately asked me to sing it again. No doubt it was because it set her thinking of her own long-dead grandmother Liza Alice McGirr (neé Cassidy).

My parents were married in 1941 in the Sacred Heart Church in Omagh, following which the wedding party adjourned to Bundoran, some fifty miles (or 80 kilometres) away on Donegal's Atlantic shore. Wartime petrol rationing failed to disrupt the conduct of the nuptials and their aftermath, for the couple and their guests made their way to Bundoran in a convoy of cars, my father having arranged a special stash of precious fuel to see them there and back. The honeymoon was spent in The Gaelic Hotel, Bundoran, which was a family hotel run by the Meehan family. We often visited and sometimes holidayed there in subsequent years.

George Thompson's house in Drumquin 'proper' was the scene of my birth, with Dr Joseph Campbell, one of the two local GPs, and Alice Thompson, the District Nurse, in attendance. Between 1942 and 1956, my mother bore six children. My only sister, Sheila, and my brother, Seán, were born in speedy succession in that same house. My brothers Aidan, Brendan, and Declan were hospital babies. As an infant child I was carted around in the back of my father's car in a sally-rod basket commissioned for me.

I had a wooden pedal car, specially manufactured for me. Sharing it with my sister Sheila was a fraught process at the best of times and the source of constant disagreement between us. My decision to paint this car coincided with Sheila's wish to enjoy a spell pedalling around in it and so it transpired that since she declined to vacate the vehicle, she got a coat of red paint for her trouble. Another day, we fell out about something or other and I sentenced her to a spell of detention in a shed in which the geese were kept. She was declared missing and panic set in until, hours later, I confessed to having detained her against her wishes and revealed the location of her captivity. Such evidence points to me having been a horrible child, pretty beastly at least to my only sister.

SHEILA AND SÉAMAS

I can say with certainty that I do not remember when I peed in the parish priest's pocket as Father Dougan rocked me in his arms, for I was only an infant child at the time, but that and other stories have been recounted so many times over the years that it is difficult to say what I truly remember of all that kind of thing and what I know about such escapades from frequent retellings. One time, I somehow managed to open the door handle of my father's car with my foot as it was being driven along by a long-standing employee, Frank Cassidy, and I tumbled out onto the road. That time my howling was quelled by the inspired introduction of a banana, a rare treat and probably the first I had ever seen, but I still bear slight scars from the incident. Other times, I was reprimanded, beaten on occasion round the legs with a sally rod – usually (insult being added to injury) the instrument of punishment having been plucked, by order, by my own hand.

My parents were hard-working, industrious people who enjoyed life and knocked a lot of fun out of it. They both had a good head for figures, my father being especially nimble at mental arithmetic. My mother had a flair for business and ran her own successful drapery and shoe shop for many years. She benefited hugely from the good advice and helping hand of her sister Susie who had long experience in one of Omagh's premier stores, J.B. Anderson's of Lower Market Street. My mother's shop had been established and run in Drumquin for many decades by John and Bridget Maguire, and she and my father had acquired it on their death, together with an adjacent small plot of land. On the day the shop opened for business, I remember Susie and my mother anxiously awaiting the arrival of the first client to cross the threshold and their palpable relief when this customer departed having made some small purchase or other. It would have betokened bad luck for the business had no transaction ensued and money not changed hands.

My mother was an enthusiastic knitter and, like my father and pretty well everyone else at that time, a smoker. On the day before she died at the age of 79, among the items on her list of 'messages' was an order for 100 cigarettes. For all that, they both enjoyed

MAJ WITH TERESA & JOHN O'KANE

good health for the greater part of their lives.

Both my parents were excellent card-players, my father being especially skilled at Solo, a complicated card-game like whist in which one player may oppose the others. It involves making a declaration as to the number of tricks one might win, including an option of undertaking to win no tricks at all. 'Going *misère*', as this was called, was deemed to be especially difficult and my father, being adept at counting the cards, was a dab hand at it. My sister Sheila too had wonderful hands, being a master craftswoman and quilt-maker. I fell heir to a mere vestige of his talents – namely his ambidexterity insofar as I can only deal cards with my left hand, and, if I were a boxer, would tend to be a southpaw and lead with my right; and I also dig with the left foot.

My father was active in organising pilgrimages by bus to Knock Shrine in County Mayo and on summer Sundays two or three busloads would leave for that faraway place. They would be packed to the door, often with rows of collapsible chairs up the aisle to accommodate as many pilgrims as possible. First stop was Bundoran for early morning Mass and then it was on to Sligo, Tubbercurry, and Charlestown and finally the village of Knock itself where the Blessed Virgin Mary, St Joseph, and St John the Evangelist were said to have appeared in the year 1879. Rosary after rosary was recited all the way, followed by prayers and processions and sermons on site. My father sometimes tired of all that and he and the bus drivers would adjourn to one of the very few pubs in the place to wet their whistles. A chance encounter I had there with a youth my own age (with what we called in those days 'a Free State accent') lent me a new perspective on my Irish identity when he solemnly informed me that in his opinion Northern Catholics were all the better Catholics for the bit of opposition to their beliefs they were forced to endure on their side of the border. I felt he was talking through his hat and that he was welcome to the opposition which we could have happily done without.

Had he accompanied us on the long journey home, he might have had occasion to revise his assessment of us as sterling Christians, when after a number of half-hearted rosaries from jaded pilgrims, we finally made it back to Bundoran. The pilgrimage petered out at that stage as passengers succumbed headlong to the temptations of drink and slot machines. I remember a fellow who had one too many, shouting joyously as he stumbled off the bus in Langfield – 'If I don't see youse through the week, I'll see youse through the window!'

Pilgrimages to destinations nearer to home there were aplenty too – sometimes by bus to Doon Well, in the parish of

Termon a few miles west of Letterkenny in County Donegal, and also to St Patrick's Purgatory on Lough Derg, near Pettigo in the same county, to which people occasionally made their way on foot across the hilly terrain separating Langfield from Donegal, following a mountain path called the 'Green Road'. My mother and sister Sheila were frequent visitors to 'the Island' as it was called, while my father boasted that he had driven people there many times but had never actually done the pilgrimage himself. Nor did I. 'Doing Lough Derg' was not a business for the faint-hearted under the regime that prevailed in those days with strict fasting (the black fast), all-night vigils, and doing the rounds barefoot over jagged stones around the 'beds'. I well remember exhausted female family members on the evening of their return from their ordeal sitting around the kitchen table waiting patiently for the clock to strike twelve midnight so that they could break their fast. Tough women!

We suffered the usual childhood afflictions and illnesses, but my people, despite being relatively well off, were never so far removed from their roots as to lose touch with old ways – things like traditional cures which were widely employed for sprains, burns, ringworm, and other minor ailments. I was cured of whooping cough as a child by being led three times under a donkey, for example, a process I would later come to recognize as 'passing through'– an ancient stratagem aimed at achieving the transfer of an individual from one state (ill) to another (healthy). Likewise, warts were cured by finding a black snail (without looking for it), rubbing it on the wart, and impaling it on a thorn where, like the wart, it would fade away and die.

Otherwise, as we grew older, we roamed the fields around us, and on hot summer days were allowed to swim under supervision in the river at a spot known as 'The Meetings' where two small mountain streams met and in the centre of which there

SÓC with cow near Drumquin

was supposed to be what we called a 'turnhole', a kind of whirlpool down which one might disappear never to be seen again. Generally, we did not venture far from the bank – or the 'broo' (Irish *bruach*) as we called it – but largely confined ourselves to paddling in the shallows. Another part of the river called 'The Sandy Beds' was a favourite spot for fishing for minnows with jam jars on a string. It was also the spot to which the children of some local families were shepherded for their weekly Saturday-night bath, there being no proper bathing facilities or running water in most houses at the time.

Later, I graduated to more serious fishing with home-made tackle. This consisted of a stout branch to which eyeholes were attached to accommodate a line, an empty spool with a small nail driven into it that functioned as a reel, a hook, and a cork from one of the many bottles of stout dispensed in local hostelries completed the assembly. We were always on the lookout for what we called a 'fresh' [pronounced *fraish*], that is to say a sudden flood in the river sufficiently turbulent as to cause worms to be dislodged from their hidey-holes and sent tumbling into the muddy waters. The trick was to catch the 'fresh' while it was still rising before the trout had had time to stuff themselves to the gills and consequently cease to take any interest in our offerings. Alternatively, one might hold fire until the 'fresh' had subsided and the fish began to nibble again.

*   *   *

During my school years I had a passionate interest in sport, having been a Gaelic footballer since childhood. My interest in football was nurtured by my father, himself a player in his time and a regular attendee at county matches and championship games at Croke Park where I got to see various matches including the Armagh v. Kerry All-Ireland semi-final of 1953, sitting close to the sideline in those days. I was a member of the Drumquin minor team that won the West Tyrone Minor (under eighteen) League of 1959. We were fancied to do well in the Minor championship of that year too but, following a replay, we fell at the first hurdle to Fintona.

I played full back in both matches and ranged against me at full forward was a classmate with whom I shared a school-bench. We both looked forward to the encounter and made a solemn agreement that we would play fair against one another. It did not turn out that way for, alas, my opponent's first action was to rake the studs of his boots down my shin, following which all bets were off and no quarter was given or sought.

The first encounter was played in Drumquin and was notable for the manner in which we conceded a huge half-time lead to find ourselves neck and neck with Fintona with only minutes to go. We would surely have been beaten but for the fact that the match had to be abandoned following an outbreak of fisticuffs on the sideline and subsequent pitch invasion. I remember hearing the mock battle cry 'Up Fintona for hairy butter,' set up by our supporters as the affray raged back and forth. The replay in the Christian Brothers' Park in Omagh, in which Fintona ran out easy winners, was a much tamer affair.

Later that season we were drawn against Fermanagh champions, Newtownbutler, in the first round of the Ulster Minor Club Championship. Our team was bolstered by star players from the neighbouring parishes of Dregish and Aughyaran that were unable to field GAA teams of their own at the time and we were expected to do well. We trained mightily for the match, which was played in Irvinestown, a north Fermanagh town lying a few hundred yards from the county line with Tyrone. After a heroic struggle by both sides, the match ended in a draw.

Little did I know that it was the last game I would ever play with Drumquin or any other team. On foot of notification from Gael Linn that my gold medal award ceremony was scheduled to take place in St Patrick's Hall, Armagh, on the very same evening that had been set for the replay, I decided with a heavy heart to pull out of the side. In a manner of speaking I had given up football for the Irish language, a decision I never regretted. My team-mates, however, could hardly be blamed for taking a different view, especially since we lost the replay and were eliminated from the championship.

For all that, I have retained a lifelong interest in Gaelic sport and, as my horizons expanded, other sports as well, but I never played again.

Gaelic football was the only organized team sport played in Langfield in those days; and for all that the religious and political divide yawned just as wide in our young lives as it does today, we enjoyed the fellowship of a handful of handy Protestant lads who regularly claimed their places in the team; and despite the rampant Sabbatarianism of the day, when called upon to do so, they had no objection to togging out with us on Sundays.

One of these valued players was the son of a local shopkeeper who, in deference to his largely Protestant customer base, ordained that the boy should not be seen sallying forth with his gear on a Sunday. The father had no objection, however, to him stashing his boots and togs behind a convenient hedge on a Saturday evening for discreet retrieval on the way to a match the following day. Another of these lads went on to captain the team and his photo adorns the walls of the clubhouse.

Our interest in football knew no bounds and, in addition to kick-abouts among ourselves, we longed to engage in matches with teams from outside the parish. This was easier said than done, for, at that particular time, whatever kind of formal club structures had once existed were in abeyance, and there was nothing to facilitate such arrangements. One such effort was a challenge I arranged between Drumquin and my classmates at Omagh CBS Primary School, a party of ten or twelve of whom duly arrived by the regular bus service from Omagh one Saturday.

We swiftly adjourned to a nearby field fitted with makeshift goalposts, and joined battle. Many of my classmates had never kicked a ball in their life and we won hands down despite losing one of our best players half-way through when word arrived from his mother – a woman who brooked no nonsense – that his dinner was on the table. My mother entertained us all to a meal, following which the Omagh boys took the evening bus back to town.

On another occasion, my father and a neighbour transported us all the way to Drumduff, near Beragh, to engage with a local team without status – just like ourselves. This engagement was arranged by some of my classmates at Omagh CBS Grammar School who were natives of the Drumduff district, aided and abetted by my father and Paddy Kelly of nearby Deroran, the husband of my mother's sister (and my godmother), Kathleen. The outcome was unrecorded, but the occasion will forever remain memorable for the fact that the entire Drumquin team was crammed into two cars with one young player having to be accommodated in the boot due to lack of space. My father would stop now and then to check on his condition to ensure that he survived the trip.

Things improved eventually to the point where we were able to acquire proper kit, the single most important element of which was jerseys. A local schoolteacher helped to solve the problem of financing their purchase by organizing bands of youngsters to pick rose hips growing in hedgerows of the byways of the parish. We filled bag upon bag of these and they were then despatched for sale to fund the purchase of our jerseys.

Today, the club then simply known as 'Drumquin' is called the 'Drumquin Wolfe Tones', a token, I suppose, of the politicization of parish life, including sport, in the decades of 'the Troubles'. As elsewhere in the GAA clubs nowadays, the club has developed its own grounds and clubhouse and is a focal point for sporting youth generally, but sadly without the kind of cross-community participation that was par for the course in my young days. On the other hand, some of today's young GAA players there and elsewhere enjoy participating in other sports such as soccer and rugby, often as a result of their services being sought out. Two of my nephews have worn the green jersey in rugby for Ireland Under-19s and Under-20s respectively, and one of them played for Ulster.

*   *   *

I remember the 'Big Snow' of 1947 when the whole country was brought to a standstill. In my mind's eye I see a network of pathways excavated between houses with snow piled high on either side. In later years

THE 'BIG SNOW' OF 1947

I heard stories about all kinds of heroics such as corpses of individuals who had passed away being carried on the tops of hedges until access was gained to a main road, along which the bearers struggled onwards to the burying ground. Severe winter frosts brought opportunities for making slides, especially down the steep incline at the head of Main Street where a supply of water from a standing pump swathed in straw helped to create a super slippery surface. Some foolhardy individuals resorted to making slides across a nearby small lough whose surface froze solid when temperatures plummeted.

Winter mornings could feel very chilly indeed, especially for small boys in short trousers. One day, I arrived home from school to find the place in uproar because my mother could not find her fur-lined bootees which had seemingly disappeared into thin air. Bewilderment was replaced by hilarity when it was discovered that I had appropriated them that morning and quite unabashed had worn them to school. Summer days, we loved to go barefoot, often returning to base covered in tar which had to be removed from feet and legs by generous application of butter. We also wore what we called 'gutties', a sort of downmarket tennis shoe made of gutta-percha, 'a tough greyish-black substance got from various Malaysian trees' – or so my dictionary tells me. A fancy ballroom in Enniskillen, County Fermanagh, that officially went by the name 'The Silver Sandal' was known far and wide as 'The Gutty'.

'Birling hoops' was another favourite pastime and, at certain times of the year, we never went anywhere without them, bar chapel on Sundays. Generally these were the bare rims of disused bicycle wheels, powered by judicious application of a short baton that we also used with great dexterity for turning and braking – the epitome of good birling. De luxe models – of which there were precious few – came fitted with tube and tyre, but whereas this made for greater speed and manoeuvrability, such hoops suffered the drawback of not making much of a noise while being birled along.

Sometimes, as a special treat we would trek across the hills to visit a mountain lake called Lough Lee which has a glorious sandy shore running all around it. In days gone by, the sand on which we sported was used for sharpening scythes and reaping hooks and the like. Here too, danger lurked, for we were told that it also had a turnhole that channelled its waters into a tunnel running underground for miles to emerge eventually in some far distant place.

Once a year, like most other parishes, we enjoyed the spectacle of the parish sports, the preparations for which were almost as engaging as the occasion itself. Grass-cutting, fencing, measuring courses for the various races and athletic competitions, and lining out a pitch for the seven-a-side football tournament were among the tasks feverishly undertaken by an army of volunteers on the evenings before the big day. A special attraction for me was the construction of a temporary wooden bridge over the river encircling all but a distant corner of the field, through which entrance the paying public would gain access to the proceedings. Dusk on the eve of the sports saw the erection of a tall pole – a rough spar stripped of its branches – in readiness for the flying of the tricolour on sports day – a forbidden emblem of our Irish identity under Stormont law. In those days, the tricolour took pride of place over the proscenium arch of the stage in the parochial hall, and the national anthem (which we called 'The Soldiers' Song' and the words of which were known to but a few) was always played at dances there.

A feature of the sports was the presence of marching pipe bands: our own Hibernians ('Oul' Hibs' = Ancient Order of Hibernians) in white shirts and dark trousers, and another kilted assembly of pipers on whose big drum the words

'Tulach Néill' stood out. This I later learned was the Irish for Sixmilecross, a village lying to the south of Omagh whence these pipers stemmed, but for me and most others not in the know these words might as well have traced the name of the big drummer himself.

The Tea Rooms, located in the old Creamery premises, were a focal point for many, not just because of the beverage itself and attendant sweetmeats on offer, but also the presence of a wet-battery radio set tuned to Radio Éireann or 'Athlone', as it was more widely known, and the voice of Mícheál Ó hEithir extolling the exploits of far away counties strutting their stuff in Croke Park in All Ireland semi-final matches. We cheered for whatever Ulster team happened to be trying its luck against the might of Kerry or Meath or Mayo. The strange sounding names of the players added an odd kind of glamour to the occasion. Some of the Mayo surnames were not unlike our own, but others such as Prendergast, Loftus, Langan, Gilvarry, and Mongey sounded utterly strange and outlandish to our ears.

As good a take-off of Ó hEithir's distinctive tones as you were likely to hear was the speciality of a keen sportsman and local publican, whose careful inclusion of the ritual opener in 'Irish' lent further authenticity to his delivery for an audience of his customers. The fact that the individual concerned knew no Irish posed no difficulty for he simply rattled off a sequence of nonsensical syllables that sounded for all the world like Irish and which were just as impenetrable to his listeners' ears as the real thing would have been. Well known to one and all, his bogus chant of 'a-slug-a-sloo-a-slug-a-slug–a-hone-y' was completely meaningless, of course, but utterly convincing as far as they were concerned.

It would be 1956 before Tyrone won its first Ulster Championship and proceeded to defeat at the hands of Galway in that year's semi-final. I remember seeing a balladeer on the street in Clones that day selling roughly printed versions of his songs and singing, as it appeared to me, up his sleeve, a hand affixed to one ear. The words he sang and sold bemoaned the sudden demise of a donkey that had been mistakenly gunned down by a bunch of trigger-happy B-Specials.

We engaged in what might be loosely called farming activities over the years. At various times we kept sheep, cows, pigs, hens, geese, ducks, and turkeys, and, apart from the customary range of vegetables, we had blackcurrants, gooseberries (which we called 'goosegabs'), rhubarb, and strawberries, as a consequence of which various jams and – when oranges became available – marmalades were manufactured on a mini-industrial scale. Broad beans were one of my father's favourite vegetables and remain one of mine too to the present day. Butter was churned, the hay was saved and, on at least one occasion, we grew flax and we also harvested (or 'won', to use the local phrase) the finest black mountain turf imaginable. To a greater or lesser extent we were all involved in most of these endeavours, not all of them always to our liking.

Saving the turf was a back-breaking job but it also brought the blessing of sunny days in the mountain heather above Slavin Glen (or 'Up Number Ten', as they used to say of the curiously named steep incline leading to the bog). Tea in the bog was one of the highlights as was also the odd snooze as we lounged around in between bursts of activity. No doubt to keep us on our toes, we were warned against falling asleep in the heather in case the 'mankeeper' – a newt – happened upon us. It was believed that this reptile, shaped like a small trout with four legs, was capable of sliding down one's throat, taking up residence in one's stomach, eating its fill, ultimately causing its unfortunate host to waste away and die.

A reputed cure for this distressing condition was for the host to consume neither food nor drink for three days at the end of which time he or she would devour a feed of salt herring and then adjourn to some nearby babbling brook, prostrate themselves with mouth agape and head hung over the water. Sooner or later the mankeeper would emerge to assuage its thirst thus resolving the difficulty. Once, it is said, a victim of the newt, who had been admonished to maintain his position in the prescribed manner following its exit, had the grim satisfaction of seeing the creature jump back down his throat only to re-emerge immediately carrying seven of its young.

This little anecdote about the thwarting of a thirsty newt has a wide international distribution and an ancient history. It was first documented in Irish literature a millenium or so ago, and may well have been around in oral tradition for a great deal longer than that.

It was widely believed that if you had the courage to lick the mankeeper's belly – running the risk of it grasping the opportunity to jump down your throat as you did so! – you would thereby acquire a cure for burns. A fellow parishioner of mine who, appropriately enough, was nicknamed 'The Doctor', had apparently done just that and thereby possessed this cure which he exercised by licking the affected spot with his tongue.

We kept deep litter hens at one juncture and once when my siblings and I were old enough to be left at home to 'mind the house' while our parents headed off on one of their regular jaunts to Donegal, I conceived a plan to frustrate the onset of ennui as we hung around with nothing to amuse us. I found a drop of whiskey somewhere in the house and used it to lace the hens' mash. We observed the inevitable outcome of this dastardly application with great glee as the poor, bewildered creatures tottered about the henhouse, some balancing precariously on one leg, then toppling over. Happily they all recovered quickly and seemed none the worse for my ministrations, but it could have turned out very badly indeed especially if egg production had been affected or one or more of them had died. In retrospect, I have no hesitation in saying that I deserved a whipping for that, but *omertà* prevailed and no one was ever the wiser of my wickedness.

The production of eggs was an important element of the rural economy as they were often bartered for groceries and other supplies. Consequently, Granny O'Kane's shop always had a surfeit of them and every week she would prepare these and her own eggs for boxing and subsequent collection by the 'eggman', a travelling agent who then delivered them to some central location. My graduation to assisting in helping to clean the eggs was a mark of trust as they had to be handled with great care while being rubbed energetically with a damp cloth dipped in soda. I was also allowed to help in the shop after Sunday morning Mass, measuring tea into pound and two-pound bags from a wooden tea chest and cutting ounce segments from a stick of tobacco with a razor-sharp round-headed knife. Being allowed to engage with all of this was its own reward, but Granny would also make sure that I got a 'mineral' (lemonade) and a Paris bun by way of formal compensation.

The same young curate, Father Deery, who had recruited me as an altar boy, also introduced me to the Drumquin Players, an amateur drama group specialising in what were called 'kitchen comedies'. 'Paid in His Own Coin' and 'A Damsel in Distress' are two of the titles I remember. It was an enjoyable experience though I was no actor and simply learned off my lines and repeated them as required, quite robotically I'm sure. We travelled around a bit, performing in neighbouring parish halls. One of these plays featured two ducks that took to the stage and were then shunted off again after a decent interval. These ducks were the stars of the show and country audiences loved it all. Everyone wondered at their magnificently unruffled stage presence, but the fact was that these creatures were kept on short rations for some days in advance of a performance and when fed grain on stage pecked feverishly at it the while, taking no notice of lights or laughter or anything else as they assuaged their hunger. A local schoolteacher and I once played two drunken solicitors seated with bottle and glass and imbibing cold tea as if we were enjoying it. I was severely discombobulated by a keen-eyed youngster's comment at a performance in Carrickmore: when speaking from the front row, he loudly pointed out to his mother that I was sporting a Pioneer pin in my lapel but drinking whiskey for all that!

The year 1950 which was declared a 'Holy Year' by the Catholic Church, saw my father organize a hugely more ambitious kind of pilgrimage, for he and my mother decided to visit Rome. He bought his vehicle – a brand new Vauxhall Velox – from his friend, Fred Charleton of Charleton's garage in Omagh. It was a medium-sized four-door model, registration HZ 3533, a six-cylinder saloon with a three-speed gearbox and a top speed of 75 miles per hour. Production of these cars had begun in 1949 and, in a time of post-war scarcities, they were difficult to come by. It set him back £550, but he was a moneyed man in those days and well able to absorb that outlay and the expense of the long journey through England, France, and Switzerland to Italy and the Eternal City.

It was an ambitious undertaking and one that required a great deal of forward planning, including the acquisition of basic language skills in French and Italian, neither of which had featured in my parents' schooling or that of their three passengers – my mother's sister Susie and her friend Agnes Farry, and her brother Pat. Some of that slack was taken up through the efforts of Father Devine, the local curate of the day, who gave them lessons in both languages throughout the winter of 1949 and early spring of 1950. I remember seeing the priest going about this task, his charges lined up on benches (or 'forms') before him in our front room at Omagh Road, Drumquin. Fluency in either language was never really on the cards, but learning enough to carry them through was a major achievement in itself. They used to joke about what they called 'haircut' beans (*haricot vert*) which they became thoroughly sick of eating; I fancy their mispronunciation of the only word of either tongue I ever heard any one of them utter was as much by way of registering how disagreeable they found this seemingly omnipresent vegetable offering as anything else. They must have been in receipt of advice from other quarters also in respect of detailed planning of their itinerary, accommodation, and travel documents.

In their absence, Sheila, Seán, Aidan, and I were looked after by our Cassidy grand-parents and two of my father's employees – Mickey Mimnagh and Winnie McGeehan. I do not remember much

Aidan, Seán, Séamas, & Sheila

about their departure but I vividly recall their triumphant return. They came laden with presents, including 30 pairs of rosary beads specially blessed by His Holiness and intended as gifts for the members of the workforce in my father's employ, approximately half of whom were Protestants! I often heard my mother say that the beads they had originally purchased were stolen from them by a phalanx of nuns seated behind them in St Peter's Square. Their bags were full of strange coins and million-lira paper notes and cuckoo clocks from a place called 'Switcherland', as my father always pronounced it. There was talk of snakes where they picnicked along the roadside and of the difficulty in finding decent drinking water anywhere. It was an epic journey, remarkable in its scope and execution across the continent of Europe only recently emerged from the rigours of war. It was a homecoming tinged with regret, however, for unknown to us, my mother had suffered a miscarriage on the long trek back to Ireland. My mother suffered indifferent health for a number of years after their Holy Year adventure for reasons that may have been connected with her misfortune on the homeward journey. She was hospitalized at first in the Tyrone County Hospital in Omagh and, then, for nine long months, in St John's Ward of the Mater Private Hospital in Belfast.

Young and all as I was, accounts of their travels were perhaps the spur that caused me to take for my confirmation name 'Columbanus' – the saintly Irish monk who left Ireland long ago during the Dark Ages to be 'a pilgrim for Christ' on mainland Europe. Or, perhaps, I was somehow inspired by it all to contemplate a peregrination to match theirs, as indeed I was one day to do, though in an entirely different direction.

FAMILY TREE
(FROM 1802)

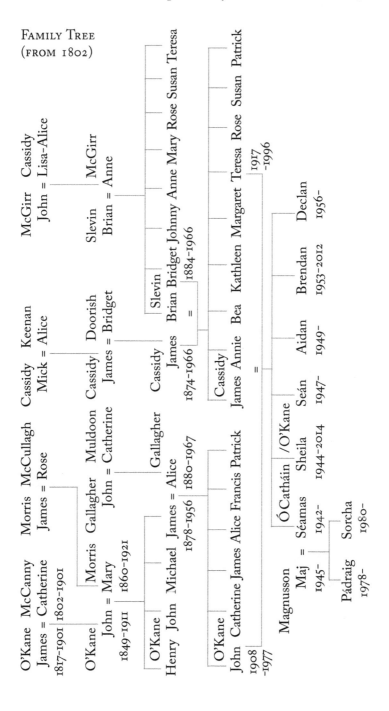

RIGHT >
SÓC AT UNIVERSITY
OF MARYLAND, 2004,
WITH *(AT FAR RIGHT)*
PEGGY BULGER, HEAD
OF FOLKLORE SECTION,
LIBRARY OF CONRESS

< LEFT
SÓC AS VICE-PRESIDENT
OF THE INTERNATIONAL
GOLDEN HARP
TELEVISION FESTIVAL
(OF FOLKLORE AND FOLK
MUSIC) IN 1984
[*PHOTO COURTESY RTÉ*]

RIGHT >
SÓC AT THE ROYAL
GUSTAVUS ADOLPHUS
ACADEMY,
UPPSALA UNIVERSITY,
SWEDEN, IN 1994

< LEFT
AT THE OPENING OF
ULSTER UNIVERSITY
ACADEMY FOR IRISH
CULTURAL HERITAGES
AT MAGEE COLLEGE,
DERRY, IN 2001:
SÓC WITH SÉAMUS
MAC MATHÚNA,
PROINSIAS MAC CANA
& SEAMUS HEANEY

THE AUTHOR

D R Séamas Ó Cathain, born in Drumquin County Tyrone in 1942 and educated at Queen's University Belfast, has been Professor of Celtic at QUB, and Professor of Irish Folklore at University College Dublin, and Director of the National Folklore Collection of UCD.

He is the author of *Uair a Chloig cois Teallaigh /An Hour by the Hearth* (Comhairle Bhéaloideas Éireann: 1985), and of *Gaelic Grace Notes* (Novus Press, Oslo: 2014). He is the editor of *Northern Lights: Following Folklore in North-Western Europe* (UCD Press: 2001), and joint editor of *Treasures of*  *the National Folklore Collection /Seoda as Cnuasach Bhéaloideas Éireann* (Four Courts Press: 2010).

He has contributed to folklore programmes broadcast by RTÉ and the BBC; in the 1980s he has been a jury member of the internationally televised Golden Harp Festival; and from 1996 to 2005 he was Editor of *Béaloideas*, the Journal of the Folklore of Ireland Society.

His many international distinctions and awards include: Knight (First Class) of the Order of the Lion of Finland in 1986; the Dag Strömbäck Prize of the Gustavus Adolphus Academy, Uppsala, Sweden, in 1994; and the Ruth Michaelis-Jena Ratcliff Prize, Edinburgh, in 1995. He is an honorary member of the Finnish Kalevala Society since 1981; a member of the Folklore Fellows of the Finnish Academy of Sciences, Helsinki, since 1990; and a sometime member of the Advisory Board of the Research Institute of Irish and Scottish Studies at the University of Aberdeen.

Living in Dublin since 1973, he is married to Maj Magnusson, whom he met in the late 1960s while he was a Lecturer in Celtic Philology and Folklore at the University of Uppsala in Sweden. They have a son Pádraig and a daughter Sorcha.

ILLUSTRATIONS

ACKNOWLEDGEMENTS

I am deeply indebted to my friend Patrick McCabe, who read the typescript in its entirety and had many suggestions to make for improvement. His interest and enthusiasm has been a constant encouragement to me. I owe him a debt of thanks too for fashioning the first contact with my publishers.

Similarly, I have to thank my wife, Maj, whose keen eye and sense of style and precision has saved the day for me on numerous occasions. I also wish to thank Des Donegan, Dr Éilís Ní Dhuibhne, and Professor Emeritus Seosamh Watson for much useful comment and advice on the content of the original typescript, and also Christina Albertini who provided advice on some linguistic matters.

This version of my story from 1942 to 1968 owes much to the brilliant interventions of Sheila Jones and John D. O'Dwyer of Phaeton Publishing and their skilled work in reshaping the order of the text and in embellishing it with photographs, maps, and drawings.

From my home place, I have to thank my sister-in-law, Ella, who supplied me with a wide range of photographic material, her husband, Seán, and their daughters, Clare and Pauline, who probed fruitlessly far and wide in pursuit of border photographs. For similar services, thanks also to my brother, Declan, his wife, Bernie, and daughter-in-law, Maria. Frank Mulryan kindly supplied the photograph of me and my schoolmates at Drumquin P.E.S.

I also wish to extend my gratitude to Torill Lindseth Wigelius and her siblings in faraway Lapland. Torill rendered my spelling of Sámi expressions in accordance with modern usage, and her childhood neighbour, Øyvind Nilsen, confirmed the identity of some individuals and locations in my Lapland photos.

Last, but not least, I wish to thank Dr Críostóir Mac Cárthaigh, Director of the National Folklore Collection at University College Dublin, for permission to access and publish archive materials, and also Jonny Dillon and other staff members of the same institution for expert assistance.

Séamas Ó Catháin, 2018

EXTREMELY ENTERTAINING SHORT STORIES
—Classic Works of a Master
by Stacy AUMONIER

576 pages: biography, 29 stories, & 1 essay
ISBNS (HBK): 9780955375651 (PBK): 9780955375637

STORIES OF WORLD WAR I & THE 1920s
'Stacy Aumonier is **One of the Best Short-Story Writers of All Time.**' —JOHN GALSWORTHY (winner of the Nobel Prize for Literature).

BROADCAST ON BBC RADIO 4 *Afternoon Readings*: '...not only hilarious, full of wit and genuine warmth for his subjects, but also beautifully constructed insights into the various absurdities of human behaviour...'—BBC *RADIO 4 PROGRAMMES*, 2011

'...a very elegant volume...short stories that invite comparison with those of Saki, O.Henry and even Guy de Maupassant.' —*BOOKS IRELAND*

'...in England...I bought the new Phaeton collection of *Extremely Entertaining Short Stories* by Stacy Aumonier... Back now in New York, it's a heavy volume to cart back and forth as subway reading, but it's well worth the weight' —*LIBRARY JOURNAL*, NEW YORK

'Aumonier could condense a life into a few pages. ...unrivalled as a short story writer ...Perfect with a hot toddy on a cold night.' —*INDEPENDENT*, LONDON

PHAETON PUBLISHING LTD. DUBLIN WWW·PHAETON·IE

FRENCH CINEMA IN CLOSE-UP
—La Vie d'un acteur pour moi
edited by Michaël ABECASSIS with Marcelline BLOCK

452 pages (royal octavo size), 180 illustrations
ISBN (PAPERBACK): 978-1-908420-114
MINI-DICTIONARY OF FRENCH CINEMA ACTORS

Chosen '**One of the 5 Best Reference Books of 2015 in the Arts**' by *LIBRARY JOURNAL*: 'There may be other biographical dictionaries of the French Cinema, but none with such engagingly written biographies as this one. ...The highlights of the dictionary are the hand-drawn caricatures by artists Jenny Batlay, New York, and Igor Bratusek, Sorbonne, that accompany each sketch. Read collectively, the pieces document trends in French cinema and its close connections with the theater.' — *LIBRARY JOURNAL*, NEW YORK

'...so rich in personal detail that it feels as if the reader is hearing the story from an old friend...its innovative format allows for a vast range of contributors...In linking French cinema to the other arts and to the history of France, the book succeeds in offering everyone who picks it up, from the veteran cinema buff to the merely curious, a chance to learn something new ...succeeds in placing French cinema in general under the magnifying glass, not just its actors...' —*BOOKS IRELAND* MAGAZINE

'...combines some of the best aspects...of academic study and coffee-table book...' —*STUDIES IN EUROPEAN CINEMA* JOURNAL

9 781908 420268